Also by Master Hsing Yun

Being Good
Lotus in the Stream
Where Is Your Buddha Nature?
Buddhism Pure and Simple

BUDDHISM
Core Ideas

BUDDHISM
Core Ideas

by Master Hsing Yun

translated by Tom Graham

New York • **WEATHERHILL** • Tokyo

First edition, 2002

Published by Weatherhill, Inc.
41 Monroe Turnpike
Trumbull, CT 06611

Library of Congress Cataloging-in-Publication Data available on request.

Contents

BUDDHISM
Core Ideas

CAUSE AND EFFECT

The law of cause and effect is central to Buddhism. It lies at the core of the Buddha's teachings on karma, dependent origination, impermanence, no-self, and emptiness. Indeed, the practice of Buddhism itself is based on this law, for if the teachings of the Buddha did not cause our lives to improve, there would be no point in learning them.

The Buddha said that all things are caused. This applies to both the physical and the mental realms. While most people today understand that all things in the physical realm are caused, they frequently do not recognize that all things in the mental realm are caused as well. And yet they are. Our dreams, memories, thoughts, and intentions all have been caused, either by sensory input, by our interactions with other people, or by the operations of our minds themselves.

When we consider intentional behavior, the law of cause and effect becomes most significant, for whenever we act intentionally we generate karmic causes that produce inevitable results. These results, which become part of our "mind stream," ultimately generate the conditions that prevail in our lives. Ultimately, they determine what sort of culture we are born into, what sort of body we have, what sort of family we are raised in, what sort of language we speak, and the kinds of things that happen to us. Good (helpful) intentions produce good results, while bad (harmful) intentions produce bad results.

Many people withdraw from the subject of cause and effect because they do not want to entertain the idea that what happens to them is their own responsibility. This is too bad, for if the law of cause and effect is properly understood, it can only help us. If there were no such law, it would not be possible for us to have been born and raised, to improve the conditions of our lives, or to realize the ultimate goals of Buddhism. The law of cause and effect is not a form of punishment and it is not administered by a supreme intelligence. It simply is. If we understand how this law works, we can use it to our advantage. If we do not understand how it works, we will surely remain at its mercy.

The *Dhammapada* says, "If we live to be one hundred years old but never come to understand the law of cause and effect, our lives will not be worth as much as if we had lived for only one day but came to understand this law."

INCORRECT VIEWS ON CAUSE AND EFFECT

Besides simply ignoring it, there are many ways of misunderstanding the law of cause and effect. These misunderstandings can be quite serious, since they may lead us to do things that bring harmful results. I will mention the most common misunderstandings below.

Divine causes, divine effects. This view says that all things are caused by gods and that if we want to improve our conditions, we have no other recourse but to appeal to these gods. Many Buddhists believe in "higher powers" or "higher beings" that can be called on in time of need. However, if we place all of our faith in such things and fail to take responsibility for our own behavior, we will never get the results we desire, for even the Buddha himself is powerless to change causes that we ourselves have set in motion.

Fate. Buddhist teachings stress the importance of understanding the law of cause and effect, but this does not in any way imply fatalism or say that our lives are conditioned by fate. It is not a Buddhist teaching that all of the causes that influence our lives are already stored within us and that only these causes determine what happens to us. Our lives are conditioned by our present behavior as well as our past actions, and thus there is no such thing as fate or destiny.

Dodging causes, or being free of them. Some people believe that if we are clever, we can avoid facing the results of our behavior or that we can somehow avoid creating causes in the first place. This is not possible. All intentional acts constitute causes that generate either good, bad, or neutral results. "An arrow once shot from a bow cannot be called back again." Rather than lead us deeper into delusion, the desire to be free of the law of cause and effect should be channeled into understanding how to use this law to our advantage.

There is no cause, though there are effects. This view says that since everything is so complex and difficult to understand, it cannot be said that anything has a discreet cause.

There are causes, but no effects. This view agrees that everything is caused, but concludes that since everything is so complex, we can never truly understand the results.

There is no cause and no effect. This view simply denies the law of cause and effect without replacing it with anything.

Most people who do not clearly understand the law of cause and effect hold mixtures of the above views or allow themselves to remain ambivalent on the subject. The workings of cause and effect are indeed difficult to comprehend, but that does not mean that we should ignore them. Rather than be daunted by this complexity, it would be better if we were humbled by it and in this humility realized that even we ourselves have come into being and continue to exist only due to a vast network of causes and conditions. Once we understand this network—even if only incompletely—we will be in a position to use it to help us change our lives for the better.

BUDDHIST VIEWS ON CAUSE AND EFFECT

The Buddha taught that all phenomena are "empty," which means that not one of them has any permanent or absolute aspect whatsoever. One way of understanding emptiness is to consider that all things are caused or supported by other things. Our bodies, for example, were "caused" by our parents and are supported by food grown by others. This food, in turn, depends on sunlight, water, soil, and so forth. If any of these causes or conditions were absent or changed, our lives would change accordingly. Once we understand that everything is like this—that everything is interconnected with other things and dependent upon them—we will be in a good position to understand that each one of these things has no intrinsic being of its own. Each of them is empty. When the concept of emptiness is related to the principle of cause and effect like this, we can see that emptiness does not mean "nothingness" or "non-existence." It means that when we look deeply at any phenomenon or thing, we find no stable essence, but only an endless chain of causes and conditions. If we contemplate this chain, we will eventually come to see that everything that we think and do produces results. In the sections that follow, I will cite some of the ways that we can think about the law of cause and effect.

Understanding the concept of cause and effect, but failing to apply it. The law of cause and effect is active at all times and in everything that we do. If we understand that all of our behavior has effects, then we are probably applying this law correctly in our lives. Some people, however, understand this law only in the abstract. Though they will agree that it is true, they treat it as a mere mental construct that does not have practical application in their lives. This is a significant misunderstanding, for the law of cause and effect continues to operate whether we are mindful of it or not.

Good causes and bad causes. It is crucial to clearly distinguish between good and bad causes, for if we do not we will plant many bad seeds and bring much suffering both to ourselves and others. Good causes, which are generated by helpful intentions, lead to the well-being of the self and others, while bad causes, which are generated by harmful intentions, lead to the opposite. The enlightenment of a Buddha is caused by the accumulation of many good actions over a long period of time. Conversely, descent into the lower realms is caused by an accumulation of bad actions. The Buddha never said that we *must* choose good over bad. Instead, he explained our options. The choice is ours to make. If we use the law of cause and effect to our advantage, many good things will result. If we use it to harm ourselves and others, much suffering will result.

Inner and outer causes. A seed carries "inner" genetic material that causes it to sprout when "outer" causes such as sunlight and water are present. Similarly, human beings are influenced by both "inner" talents and tendencies and outer circumstances. All of us have brought into this life many "inner causes" or tendencies that were developed in previous lives. In addition, we have developed new tendencies and talents in this life. A great deal of Buddhist practice is directed at getting us to identify our good and bad tendencies and to use our good ones to overcome our bad ones. At the same time, we all exist within a complex network of outer causes and conditions. The ways that we choose to attend to these outer causes and conditions profoundly influence our inner talents and tendencies. For example, when frustrating conditions cause us to respond with anger and irritation, we only strengthen the inner tendencies that brought about these conditions in the first place. Conversely, when we respond to frustrating outer conditions with patience and understanding, we strengthen our inner tendencies of wisdom and tolerance, thereby lessening the chances that those outer conditions will appear again. The Buddha said, "If you want to understand your past lives, look at the conditions of your life today. If you want to understand your future lives, look at what you are doing today." Rather than feel dismayed when faced with difficult outer conditions, we should draw on our best inner tendencies and use them to change our lives for the better.

Productive and counterproductive causes. If we become ill, we will want to understand the cause of our illness and its treatment. If our understanding is correct, we will be able to find "productive causes" that will bring about a cure. If our understanding is not correct, however, we may undertake a "counterproductive cure" that will only cause our disease to worsen. This same general distinction applies to the mind. If we are unable to identify our bad tendencies or do not know what to do about them once we have, we will be unlikely to find a cure for them. Productive cures for harmful mental tendencies can be found throughout the teachings of the Buddha, for all of his talks were aimed at helping people understand themselves, and in the light of this understanding, to choose the most productive "cure."

We create our own causes and results. Many people instinctively react negatively to the idea that their spiritual growth and development is entirely in their own hands, but it is. While it is beneficial for us to appeal to the great bodhisattvas in times of need, it is also important to realize that though they may help us, there is nothing that they can do to overturn the law of cause and effect. Similarly, our teachers and mentors may provide us with good advice and good opportunities, but they cannot do much more than that. The rest is up to us. If we do not follow their advice or put their teachings into practice, we will fail to generate the kinds of causes that lead to spiritual growth.

People often react negatively to the law of cause and effect because it feels like a trap or a punishment. Rather than use this law to overcome their problems, they attempt to ignore it. Ignoring the law of cause and effect may give rise to a temporary, muddled state of pleasure, but it will never produce the lasting joy that comes from understanding how our thoughts and deeds lead to inevitable results. The Buddha did not create the law of cause and effect. He simply taught how it operates. It is one of the deepest conditions of our lives. The three poisons that give rise to all delusion are greed, anger, and ignorance. Ignorance of this law results only in an increase and continuation of delusion, while understanding it and knowing how to use it will result ultimately in our enlightenment.

CAUSES OF THE CYCLE
OF BIRTH AND DEATH

S entient beings travel from one life to the next, through many incarnations, in a journey called the cycle of birth and death. The ultimate goal
of Buddhist practice is liberation from this cycle. The root cause of our
being trapped within the cycle of birth and death is clinging to a false sense
of self. Once this "self" comes to believe in the importance of its own
desires and needs, it perpetuates the cycle of birth and death by engaging
in acts of greed, anger, ignorance, pride, and doubt.

Buddhist sutras compare the cycle of birth and death to quicksand, a
long night, an ocean, a wheel, and clouds. They say that it is like quicksand
because once we step into it, it is very difficult to get out again. They compare it to a long night because it is dark and filled with insubstantial dreams
that will evaporate upon our awakening. It is compared to an ocean because
oceans are vast and we can become completely lost if we lose our bearings
while on them. It is like a wheel because once it has begun to turn it continues to roll. Lastly, the cycle of birth and death is compared to a cloud
because it has no definite form and because it obscures the moon that is
our awakened mind.

KLESHAS

As we journey through the cycle of birth and death, most of us notice
that some sorts of thought and behavior lead to the elevation of con-

sciousness, while other sorts lead to its decline. The teachings of the Buddha will lead us to higher levels of awareness if we follow them. If we do not, we will very likely find ourselves being drawn deeper into delusion by our habits, negative tendencies, and self-defeating behaviors. Negative traits that lead to the creation of bad karma and the perpetuation of the cycle of birth and death are called *kleshas* in Sanskrit. In English they are called "defilements," "obstructions," "impurities," "obscurations," or "harmful fixations."

All delusion arises out of our kleshas. Delusion, in turn, causes us to do things that generate karma. Karma produces results that we feel and that cause us to react, often in much the same way that generated the karma in the first place. This cycle produces endless suffering for sentient beings trapped in it, for it is a self-perpetuating cycle, a perpetual-motion machine that creates its own fuel. If we can become aware of what it is that generates delusion, we will find it much easier to free ourselves from it.

There are many ways of understanding what kleshas are and how they work. Sometimes they are described as a "torpor that follows us everywhere," because their subtle negative influence can be found in almost everything that we do. They can be thought of as "shackles" or "bonds" because they bind us to our habits and prevent our acquiring better traits. Or they can be thought of as "covers" because they hide our own best interests from us. Sometimes kleshas are called "leaks" or "outflows" because they tempt us to flow out of our natural state of goodness into the world of delusion through one or more of the six senses.

Though there are many different kinds of kleshas, Buddhist tradition recognizes that just six of them—greed, anger, ignorance, pride, doubt, and wrong views—are fundamental to all deluded thought and behavior. These six kleshas are sometimes called the "fundamental kleshas" or the "bases of delusion" since all other negative spiritual traits can be traced back to one or more of these defilements. The *Treatise on the One Hundred Dharmas* says, "The six basic kleshas are greed, anger, ignorance, pride, doubt, and wrong views. These six are considered to be the most basic kleshas because they are very stubborn and give rise to all manner of physical and mental suffering. They cause great anxiety and give rise to many other secondary kleshas." In the sections below, we will look briefly at each of these defilements.

GREED

Greed is characterized by excess. When our desires become so strong they cause us to lose sleep, exercise bad judgment, behave immorally, or strain our systems, we can be sure that we are being swept away by the swift current of greed. Buddhist sutras contain many metaphors that can help us understand greed. They say that greed is like swiftly moving water, for it can quickly overwhelm us and cause us to drown. They say that it is like a nervous disease that keeps our systems overstimulated and thus makes us anxious, unable to relax, and ultimately sad. They say that it is like a flood that can sweep us into the bitter sea of suffering or that it is like a yoke that binds us to our lower urges and forces us to work like draft animals or slaves.

The *Treatise on the Stages of Yoga Practice* says that excessive desire or greed arises from clinging to the five skandhas or to mental constructs concerning either the past, present, or future. The treatise says that greed may also arise due to bad behavior, sexual desire, family and friends, possessions, and the hope that things will either continue as they are or change. Since desire is so much a part of being human, we can assume that we will find it present in nearly everything that we do.

Greed or excessive desire can also interrupt our meditation. The *Explication on the Stages of the Paramita of Samadhi* says that meditative states may be disturbed by three fundamental kinds of desire—sexual attraction brought on by the thought of someone, sexual attraction brought on by the image of someone suddenly appearing in the mind, or any other kind of desire brought on by anything else in the world. Since the meditative states bring us closer to our core emotions, it is not surprising that sexual distractions can become so prominent in meditation.

The *Treatise on the Perfection of Great Wisdom* says, "It is hard to overcome greed, but we can learn to distance ourselves from it by taking pleasure in good things. It is difficult to free ourselves from lust, and yet we can learn to break its bonds by contemplating the impermanence of the physical form."

ANGER

The *Treatise on the Perfection of Great Wisdom* says that anger is like "fire on a flammable surface." Once it has been ignited, it is difficult to stop. The treatise also says, "Anger is the worst of all defilements ... and the most difficult mental disease to cure." Anger is dangerous in and of itself, but like a wildfire, its consequences can be truly terrible, for once it has begun, as the ancients used to say, its "flames can burn down an entire forest of virtue." The ancients also said, "When a single thought of anger arises, a million doors of delusion swing open."

Once it has arisen, anger is difficult to control. If we are mindful of our feelings, however, anger can usually be stopped in the first instant of its appearance. If you feel anger rising, do not say anything and do not give in to it. If you want to speak in anger to someone, wait twenty-four hours before you do. In that time, most anger will have subsided and the situation will look very different. If you are often beset with angry feelings, contemplate the life of the Buddha and remember that all civilized behavior is founded on forgiveness and the willingness to grow beyond what we perceive as offenses against us. Anger is a powerful emotion largely because it is so uncomplicated and so easy to arouse. As Buddhists, we should turn to the wonderful virtues of patience, compassion, and tolerance whenever we are tempted by anger, for as the *Ekkotarika-agama* says, "People do not perceive the nirvana of all Buddhas due only to the flames of their anger."

IGNORANCE

The *Treatise on the Perfection of Great Wisdom* says, "When the little mind is out of touch with the Buddha mind, the thoughts that arise are called ignorance." Ignorance can be compared to darkness, numbness, drunkenness, poor eyesight, or confusion. Ignorance is the first of the twelve nidanas and the root cause of the cycle of birth and death. The *Awakening of Faith in the Mahayana* says that there are two basic kinds of ignorance—original ignorance and secondary ignorance. Original ignorance is sometimes also called "beginningless ignorance," since its origins lie not in time but in the qualities of our minds. Secondary ignorance includes all of the many harmful and confused thoughts and feelings that arise out of original ignorance. Ignorance begins with a single thought that cleaves to the deluded self rather than to the awakened Buddha within. It arises in minds that simply do not know any better.

Mind Only Buddhists say that ignorance is a quality like sleepiness or torpor and that it follows us from life to life and colors nearly everything we do. The hold that ignorance has on us is difficult to break largely because it enfeebles us and causes us to have a dull understanding of our conditions. Mind Only Buddhists also compare ignorance to shackles that constrain our movements and do not allow us to defend ourselves from our own defilements. Buddhist sutras sometimes say that ignorance is the father of delusion, while passionate clinging is the mother. These "parents" give rise to the karma that fuels the cycle of birth and death.

PRIDE

Pride is a harmful corruption of the normal desire for social approval or respect. The *Abhidharma-kosha* contains an interesting section that identifies seven kinds of pride. The first is "basic pride," the tendency to look down on others whose talents may not be as developed as our own or to under-estimate others whose talents are the same as our own. The second is "excessive pride," or the tendency to look down on others whose talents are equal to or greater than our own. The third is "extreme pride," or the tendency to look down on others whose talents are much greater than our own. The fourth is "pride of self," or the belief that the false self is better or more important than anything or anyone else. The fifth is "pride of overes-timation," or the belief that one has attained levels of achievement that one has not. The sixth is the "pride of low self-esteem," which means that one avoids others that one believes are more talented or accomplished than oneself and does not seek to learn from them due to feelings of low self-worth. The seventh is "perverse pride," which means that one has a high opinion of oneself even though one can point to no accomplishment or talent to support this claim.

Pride stifles learning and prevents us from growing beyond stages of development that we have already reached. Pride encourages us to rest on our laurels and stop learning new things. It is most easily countered by having a "beginner's mind" and approaching all situations as if they held many new and unpredictable elements, which in truth, all situations actually do. As Buddhist practitioners we must guard against all forms of pride, but especially against the "pride of low self-esteem," for this kind of attitude will cause us to turn away from precisely those people who have the most to offer us. All of us should learn to admire others, for as long as we bask in the glow of admiration we will be free of pride and open to growth.

Right views are the first aspect of the Noble Eightfold Path. The Buddha placed them first because everything that we think, say, and do follows from our views of life in this world. If our views are seriously in error, we will make many serious mistakes. If our views are more in accord with reality, we will tend to grow and prosper both materially and spiritually. Buddhist literature generally identifies five fundamental wrong views. The first is "the view of the body," or the belief that the body is the foundation of sentient life and that the realities of sentient life can only be explained in terms of the body. Though our six senses do find expression through the physical body, the Buddha taught that the body arises only after the five skandhas have come together and that the five skandhas are a more basic level of reality.

The second kind of wrong view mentioned in Buddhist literature is a "one-sided view," or any belief that emphasizes one part of the truth at the expense of the whole. For example, if we emphasize the impermanence of the physical body to the point that we become nihilists, then we will have formed a one-sided view. If we emphasize the continuance of the mind stream as it flows from one incarnation to another to the extent that we come to believe in an eternal soul, then we will have formed an opposite sort of one-sided view, often called "eternalism." The truth lies between these two views. Similarly, if we say either that the Buddha became nothing after his enlightenment or that he became something after his enlightenment, we will again be falling into the trap of one-sidedness, for the enlightenment of a Buddha cannot be described in such simple terms. A third example of a one-sided wrong view might be over-emphasizing either asceticism or sensory indulgence in our practice of the Dharma, which properly follows the "middle way" between these two extremes. One-sided views can be very detrimental to reaching a complete understanding of the teachings of the Buddha, for many of the most important points made by Shakyamuni Buddha contain subtleties that if misapprehended can lead to serious misinterpretations. This is especially true since the truths taught by the Buddha almost always contain several different levels and will be perceived by us differently at different times in our lives and at different stages of our practice.

The third kind of wrong view is called a "perverse view" or a "twisted view." Perverse views are views that contradict such fundamental truths as the four noble truths, cause and effect, karma, impermanence, or emptiness. They often lead to pride and negative behavior, since people who hold these kinds of views generally do not see any reason why they should not do whatever they want to do whenever they want to do it. The fourth kind of wrong view is called a "derivative view." Derivative wrong views are secondary beliefs that are founded upon a primary wrong view. For example, if we believe that the body alone is real, we may further develop the derived wrong view that satisfying the desires of the body is the sole purpose of life. The fifth kind of wrong view is called the "view of morality," and it arises whenever we follow harmful moral guidelines or become rigid or "moralistic" by clinging to the letter of moral rules without compassionately understanding the deep principles that underlie them.

DOUBT

The most serious form of doubt is to doubt the Buddha's teachings or to have no confidence in them. The Buddha never asked anyone to believe what he said without testing it for themselves, but if we have so many doubts that we do not even bother to test his teachings, then we will be very unlikely to gain anything from them, much less to discover the truth for ourselves. Confidence in the Dharma is important at every level of growth, for no sooner do we reach one insight, then it is time to strive for another. For example, we may gain the insight that all things are impermanent, but doubt that this applies to ourselves and thus not understand the full significance of the Buddha's teachings on emptiness. If our doubt is very strong, it may cause us to adopt the one-sided wrong view that since life is impermanent, we can and should do whatever we want. A second example might be that though we may understand much of the Buddha's teachings on the emptiness of the self, we may doubt the significance of his teachings on compassion and thus adopt the wrong view that Buddhist practice is based on escaping life in this world. All Buddhist practitioners have questions, and these questions are good and should be asked and answered, but when our questions close doors and lead us away from the Dharma, they become the klesha of doubt.

The *Treatise on the Perfection of Great Wisdom* says, "When we doubt, we do not seek the true characteristics of things. Doubt arises from ignorance and thus is evil in the midst of evil. . . . If you doubt too much, the king of death will hunt you down as easily as a lion catching a deer."

CONCLUSION

Enlightenment cannot be described in any language. The Buddha defined nirvana as simply the "extinction" of suffering or delusion because enlightened reality is so different from what we normally see and feel that there is no way we can use our ordinary minds to comprehend it. It is as if we were huddled in a dark cave and had never seen light or known freedom of movement. How is the Buddha to describe sunlight to us? How is he to describe the freedom of movement we will experience once we have left the cave? If he tells us that light resembles the sparks that arise when we rub our eyes, will that really help us understand? If he tells us that the freedom to run resembles stretching our legs in the dark, will that convince us to get up and leave the cave? Metaphors sometimes can inspire us by comparing something we know to something we do not know, but in the case of enlightenment, positive metaphors are more likely to cause us to use our minds to diminish the goal of Buddhist practice or to imagine that we understand it when we do not. The cycle of birth and death can be compared to existence within a dark cave. The teachings of the Buddha are designed to help us get up from the floor and leave the cave. The tunnel is dark and long, but if we closely follow the Buddha's instructions, we will find our way out. The Buddha's teachings on kleshas were designed to lead us out of the cave of birth and death. To lead us from darkness to light and from confinement to freedom.

THE EIGHTEEN REALMS

The Buddha divided all sentient life into two main categories—form and mind. The realm of forms includes all conditioned dharmas, everything that we think of as the material world, the physical body, and all sensory information that comes from the material world and influences the mind. The realm of the mind includes the six consciousnesses of sight, hearing, smell, taste, touch, and the thought processes that coordinate these. The realm of forms is sometimes called the "objective realm," while the realm of mind is called the "subjective realm." The enlightened mind of a Buddha is one that has so thoroughly penetrated both of these realms that the subjective and objective have merged completely and become a transcendent whole that is greater than the sum of its parts.

The Buddha's explanation of the eighteen realms describes in a general way all sensory and mental experience within this world. The eighteen realms include the *six roots*, the *six objects*, and the *six consciousnesses*, for a total of eighteen. The six roots are our sense organs—eyes, ears, nose, tongue, body, and mind. The six objects are the things perceived by these organs, or the kinds of information perceived by these organs. The six consciousnesses are the six kinds of awareness associated with these six "realms." The word realm means "kind" or "type," and thus the eighteen realms include all kinds or types of phenomena that can be perceived or cogitated by human beings

The Buddha's explanation of the eighteen realms resembles his five skandha explanation in that both of these analyses were designed to show sentient beings how their minds become attached to delusion and why they stay that way. Since it is composed of familiar elements that can be readily comprehended, the eighteen realms description of our attachment to delusion is traditionally thought to be easier to understand than the five skandha explanation, though modern readers familiar with psychological theory may well find the five skandha explanation simpler since it is composed of fewer terms.

THE SIX ROOTS

The six roots are the eye, ear, nose, tongue, body, and root of awareness (the brain and nervous system). They are the sense organs that correspond to the six senses of sight, hearing, smell, taste, touch, and the thought processes that coordinate these. The six roots are part of the rational, objective universe in that they follow natural laws and are not themselves capable of subjectivity. They are described as having both "outer" and "inner" aspects. The outer aspect is the physical organ that we can perceive with our eyes, while the inner aspect is the nerves and cells that allow the outer organ to perform its function. Both the inner and the outer aspects of the roots must be functioning for the root to provide information to the mind.

The six roots are said to have the three capabilities of limited autonomy, perception, and augmentation. *Limited autonomy* means that to some degree each root can function on its own without being directed by the mind. *Perception* means that each root has the ability to sense the world in some way. *Augmentation* means that each root provides information that augments, or adds to, the information available to the mind and that each root allows the mind to draw distinctions among phenomena. The "mind" referred to here is the sixth root, which also has the three capabilities of limited autonomy, perception, and augmentation, though in the mind's case these capabilities must be understood slightly differently from those of the other five roots since the mind is capable of extended thought, feeling, memory, and decision-making.

The *Abhidharma-kosha* says that the first five of the six roots serve to adorn sentient beings, to guide them, to provide information to the mind, and to work in concert with each other, though the realm of each root is quite distinct from the others. The sixth root—the mind—has the ability to distinguish and coordinate the information obtained through the first five roots. It also has the ability to make decisions based on that information and upon its own thoughts. When properly trained, then, the mind has the capacity to choose between delusion and enlightenment.

THE SIX OBJECTS

The six objects are called the "six kinds of dust" in Chinese. They are the objects of sensory perception, or the "realms" perceived by the sense organs. They are called "dusts" because they cloud the mind and are composed of dust-like heaps of information that are evanescent and insubstantial. The six objects are visual forms, sounds, smells, tastes, things felt by the sense of touch, and the thought patterns that result from or coordinate these sensations. These six objects are a significant part of delusion since the delusive energies of greed, anger, and ignorance nearly always find expression through them. For this reason, they are sometimes also called the "six thieves," the "six downfalls," or the "six follies."

The realm of sight comprises all data discerned by the eye, including colors, shapes, sizes, lengths, widths, proportion, direction, and so on. The realm of sound comprises all noises discerned by the ear. These noises are said to have qualities that are soft, harsh, mild, melodic, dissonant, frightening, pleasant, harmful, and so on. The realm of odor comprises all data discerned by the nose—pleasant, unpleasant, mild, and strong aromas. The realm of taste comprises all data discerned by the tongue—bitter, salty, sweet, bland, and vinegary flavors. The realm of touch comprises all data discerned by the skin—hardness, softness, wetness, motion, heaviness, lightness, slipperiness, stickiness, cold, heat, and male and female contact. The realm of thought works with all of these sensations and perceptions, evaluating, discriminating, categorizing, and judging them. (Sometimes, of course, the eye, ear, nose, and tongue may also perceive the qualities of contact associated with the skin.)

THE SIX CONSCIOUSNESSES

The six consciousnesses are the kinds of awareness associated with each of the six roots. These are seeing, hearing, smelling, tasting, touching, and thinking. Sometimes the six consciousnesses are also called eye consciousness, ear consciousness, nose consciousness, tongue consciousness, body consciousness, and thought consciousness. The first five of the six consciousnesses sense the things of the objective world, while the sixth discriminates among those things and makes decisions based upon the information it receives. The sixth consciousness is capable of making good, bad, and neutral decisions depending upon its tendencies and understanding.

The first five of the six consciousnesses exist wholly within the realm of conditioned dharmas. The sixth consciousness, since it is largely dependent on the first five, exists mainly within the realm of conditioned dharmas, and yet it is capable of rising above them. If it were not, enlightenment would not be possible.

The operation of the first five of the six consciousnesses is fairly straightforward, as is the operation of the sixth consciousness when it is solely concerned with coordinating information obtained from the first five. When the sixth consciousness acts more or less independently of the other consciousnesses, however, some further distinctions are called for. If the sixth consciousness is engaging in fantasies, harmful plans, nursing anger, or doing anything else that promotes ignorance, it will generate bad karma and keep all of the six roots bound to the cycle of birth and death. In contrast, if the sixth consciousness turns toward helping others, acquiring wisdom, studying the Dharma, or performing other wholesome activities, it will generate good karma and start freeing the six roots from their bondage to the cycle of birth and death. (This idea is discussed in depth in chapter 7.) The sixth consciousness is the turning point between good and bad, between helping others or harming them, between enlightenment and delusion.

TRAITS OF THE SIXTH CONSCIOUSNESS

Mind Only Buddhists have analyzed the sixth consciousness in great detail. In this section we will discuss some of the most prominent traits of this important decision-making part of the mind. All of the traits and capacities discussed in this section are known as "interactive" capacities, since each of them interacts with the objective world and with the mind itself. Each of them has the capacity to lead the mind either out of delusion or more deeply into delusion. While there is no need to memorize these capacities, it is good to consider them, for anything that makes us more aware of the operation of our minds will lead us closer to wisdom. In all, fifty-one traits or capacities will be mentioned in this section. They are divided into six groups.

The first group is made up of what is known as the "general capacities." These are contact, the ability to form intentions, sensation, perception, and thought. In themselves, these capacities are neutral—they are neither good nor bad. They are the basis upon which all of the rest of the interactive capacities rest.

The second group is made up of the "discriminating capacities." These are desire, understanding, formation of memory, concentration (samadhi), and wisdom. These capacities can be used either for good or bad. They are the principal decision-making tools of the mind.

The third group is made up of the "good capacities" of confidence (or faith) in the Dharma, shame, remorse, the absence of greed, the absence of anger, the absence of ignorance, diligence, tranquility, the absence of laziness, non-attachment, and harmlessness. These are the traits that lead us away from delusion and toward enlightenment.

The fourth group is made up of the six "troubling tendencies" (kleshas) of greed, anger, ignorance, pride, doubt, and wrong views. These are the six "root kleshas" that are the deep source of all delusion.

The fifth group is made up of the "tendencies that follow the six kleshas." These are the subtle ways that the six kleshas find expression in human behavior. They are subdivided into three categories—small, medium, and large. The small category gets its name from the idea that the tendencies it includes are "small" because they more or less exist by themselves. These tendencies are resentment or indignation, secretiveness, stinginess, jealousy, meanness, ill-will, hatred, flattery, deception, and arrogance. The medium category includes only two tendencies—lack of remorse and lack of shame. This group gets its name from the idea that these tendencies are almost always present when people behave badly, though they do not of themselves create bad behavior. The large category gets its name from the idea that the tendencies it includes are pervasive states of mind or attitudes that have the potential to influence everything that we do. This group includes indolence, laziness, lack of faith in the Dharma, muddle-headedness, inattentiveness, lack of mindfulness, confusion, and wrong understanding.

When the *Flower Garland Sutra* says, "The mind is a painter. It paints its own world," it is largely describing the sixth consciousness, which carries within it the capacity for both good and evil. The second noble truth of Buddhism says that the fundamental cause of all suffering is clinging to a false or deluded self. Once the sixth consciousness begins to liberate itself from its own tendency to cling to this false notion that has arisen within itself, it will begin to experience joy and tranquility. If this process of liberation continues, its sense of joy and tranquility will grow apace, for when the mind bases itself on the reality of its true condition, it frees itself from the confining limitations of selfhood and the narrowed consciousness that results from accepting that illusion.

THE THREE REALMS

The general realm of delusion in which sentient beings live is often called *samsara*, a Sanskrit word that literally means "journeying." The word samsara connotes the cycle of birth and death and the tendency for sentient beings to be reborn in delusion life after life after life. Samsara can be divided into three subrealms, which are usually called the "three realms." Understanding these three realms provides us with another way to view the six consciousnesses and comprehend how they function.

The three realms of samsara are the desire realm, the form realm, and the formless realm. The ordinary human mind functions almost exclusively within the desire realm, wherein greed, anger, ignorance, pride, and doubt rule. Desire here means both attraction and aversion, and thus fear, worry, anxiety, sadness, depression, anguish, and so on are also characteristics of this realm.

The second of the three realms, the form realm, is characterized by the presence of forms amidst the complete absence of all attraction or aversion for them. Human beings become aware of the form realm the instant their minds become desireless. Most of us experience this realm not so much as a realm of desirelessness or of forms per se, but as an ocean of tranquility that suddenly washes over us as we meditate, complete a complex task, or suddenly enter into a deeper understanding of life. We perceive this realm as tranquil and immensely satisfying for as long as we are in it, and we are free of the turbulence of fear and longing that constantly pummels the mind while it is in the realm of desire. Entry into the form realm marks entry into the first of the eight meditative states described by the Buddha (see chapter 6). The "forms" of this realm are any and all objects of perception or cognition—sights, sounds, smells, tastes, memories, dreams, sensations, and so on.

The third of the three realms, the formless realm, is marked by both the absence of all desire and the absence of all forms. This realm is entered in deep meditative states (the last four of the eight samadhis), in deep conscious sleep states, or occasionally during moments of profound relaxation. The formless realm is a state of awareness marked by the absence of all desire, all thought, all language, all imagery, all memory, and all traces of phenomenal perception. This realm is one of pristine consciousness, of pure awareness undisturbed by any cognitive or perceptual focus. Though attaining this realm, or this level of awareness, is one of the principal goals of Buddhist meditation practice, the formless realm should not be confused with enlightenment or Buddhahood, for this realm "simply" comprises the deepest strata of the sixth consciousness. Enlightenment or Buddhahood lies beyond even this.

THE FIVE SKANDHAS

The Buddha's explanation of the five skandhas is intended to help us understand the emptiness of the self. It is a short explanation aimed at his most perceptive students. The five skandhas are form, sensation, perception, activity, and individual consciousness.

The Sanskrit word *skandha* means "heap" or "aggregate" in English. The five skandhas are the "heaps" of psycho-perceptual data that fill our minds and create the illusion of a separate self. Viewed from our normal observational distance, the skandhas create and uphold the more or less ordinary illusion of an ordinary mind behaving in ordinary ways. Viewed up close and in detail, however, the skandhas appear almost like dust storms or snowstorms within the mind, for each skandha (or heap) is made up of thousands of swirling bits of information. The skandhas can also be compared to pixels on a computer screen or the dots in a pointillist painting—when viewed from a distance they produce a well-integrated image with relatively smooth contours (an image of the self), while when viewed up close they appear as a rich mosaic filled with numerous tiny details.

The term skandha can be used either microscopically to designate a single instant of perception (a single pixel or pointillist dot) or macroscopically to designate a general aspect of perception (a section of a painting or computer screen) that is dominated by one or more of the five skandhas. To view the details within an image in a painting or on a computer screen, we must hold that image still and magnify it. To view the intricate details of the skandhas, we must learn to follow the operations of our minds very closely, for the psycho-perceptual bits of data that make up the skandhas are not static, but dynamic; that is, they appear only in time. In a single instant, dozens of skandhas appear and disappear. Each skandha follows the one before and each one generates more skandhas. Viewed in this way, the skandhas might be compared to sparks in a fireworks display—each spark spins and revolves with great rapidity, and yet the patterns that all of the sparks produce appear to endure over time. When we examine the minutiae of a single skandha, we are examining a single instant on the trajectory of a single spark in a fireworks display. When we examine the patterns left by the skandhas, we are examining the world we see and live in, the "heaps" of our impressions.

The *Abhidharma-mahavibhasa Shastra* says, "In one day there are 6,400,099,980 *ksana* during which each of the five skandhas arises and is extinguished." A ksana is a unit of time. This quote refers to the minutiae of the skandhas as they appear in the moment. The following quote, from the *Great Commentary on the Five Skandhas*, refers to the "heaped" macroscopic illusions that are founded upon these minutiae. The *Commentary* says, "Why did the Buddha teach the five skandhas? He taught them to help us cure three forms of delusion and all that follows from them. The three forms of delusion are: the delusion of having a self-nature, the delusion of having a self that perceives, and the delusion of having a self that acts." The *Treatise on the Completion of Truth* makes a similar point when it says, "The sense of self that arises with the five skandhas is based on the body and the belief that the body is real. In truth, there is no self within the skandhas and that is why they are called the conditioned skandhas."

In some Buddhist texts the five skandhas are called the "five covers" because they cover our minds and prevent us from seeing deep levels of reality. In other texts they are called the "five yin (versus yang)" because they cloud the mind and hide the truth from us. I will discuss each of the five skandhas in the sections below.

THE SKANDHA OF FORM

The first skandha is form (*rupa-skandha*). Form, in this case, means anything that leads to, or is capable of leading to, the next skandha. Forms can be visual, auditory, tactile or olfactory. They can be dreams, memories, feelings, or moods. Forms are often described as being "obstructions" because, though they may lead to complex thought and activity, they are also hindrances to mental clarity since the activity they lead to is essentially deluded. It is important to remember that the five-skandha explanation is an explanation of the deluded mind and its thought processes.

The *Abhidharma-mahavibhasa Shastra* categorizes the skandha of form into three types: visible forms with a referent in the outer world such as color, size, length, position, shape, and so on; invisible forms with a referent in the outer world that are associated with the other sensory organs such as sounds, smells, tastes, and the sensations arising from physical contact; and invisible forms with no referent in the outer world such as dreams, memories, thoughts, feelings, and so on. Though a dream may be "visible" to the dreamer, it is called "invisible" here because no one else can see it. This last category of forms is associated with what the Buddha called "mental dharmas."

THE SKANDHA OF SENSATION

The second skandha is sensation (*vedana-skandha*). Following the appearance of a form, the mind reacts to it with a sensation that is either positive, negative, or neutral. We either like it, don't like it, or are neutral about it. The skandha of form arises from the union of one of the six consciousnesses with its corresponding realm. The skandha of sensation senses this union or "takes it in." This skandha "receives" forms. This is the beginning of the reification of forms (all of which are essentially empty). Though it is possible to become conscious of this skandha as it arises, most of us, most of the time, are not.

Sensations are generally categorized into two types: sensations of the body coming from the outside world through any of the sensory organs, such as sights, sounds, smells, tastes, and so on; and sensations of the mind, which may or may not come from the outside world. These include moods, feelings, memories, dreams, thoughts, ideas, and so on.

Both kinds of sensation are, of course, based on the prior appearance of a form. Greed and anger have their roots in the skandha of sensation, for if we enjoy a positive sensation we are likely to become greedy about it, while if we do not enjoy it, we are likely to become "angry" or irritable concerning it. Greed is "excessive attraction" to a sensation that we deem to be agreeable or positive, while anger (or hatred) is "excessive aversion" to a sensation that we deem disagreeable or negative. Neutral sensations often are the result of our ignorance or lack of understanding, though as we progress in Buddhist practice they may also be the result of wisdom.

Positive and negative sensations associated with the body are generally considered to be weaker than those associated with the mind, though both types of sensations often are interrelated. An example of this mixture and distinction might be a light slap in the face. While the physical sensation is only mildly unpleasant, the mental sensation will be quite strong in most cases. And yet both are interrelated.

THE SKANDHA OF PERCEPTION

The third skandha is perception (*samjna-skandha*). This skandha refers to the deepening of a sensation. It is the point where the mind begins to latch onto its sensations. At this point conscious recognition of form and sensation normally begins. It is possible to become conscious of the first and second skandhas as they are occurring, but most of us generally are not. During the skandha of perception we begin making conscious distinctions among things.

In this stage of awareness, the mind focuses on something, such as a visual image, a sound, a memory, or a sudden flight of fancy. This mental focus is a mental act akin to "selecting" something—out of the many impressions contending for its attention, the mind "selects" one. Out of the many sparks produced by the first and second skandhas, the skandha of perception selects just one. The *Samyuktabhidharma-hrdaya Shastra* says that the mind "selects an image from a realm" during the skandha of perception. The *Commentary on the Five Skandhas* says that during the skandha of perception "perceptions are selected from the realms." The *Great Commentary on the Five Skandhas* says that the skandha of perception has the "ability to add, to overrule, and to select perceptions from all realms." Since mind is the basis of the realms from which it is "selecting" its perceptions, this skandha is sometimes also said to be the skandha wherein perceptions are made or manufactured.

The *Sutra of the Great Magnificence* compares this skandha to a mirage. From a distance it looks like water, but as we approach, we find that nothing is there. The skandha of perception turns the mind toward delusion. And yet, the closer we examine that delusion, the less we find.

THE SKANDHA OF ACTIVITY

The fourth skandha is activity (*samskara-skandha*). This skandha refers to the complex mental or physical activity that often follows upon the skandha of perception. Once we have identified (perceived) something, long trains of mental associations become active. Our bodies may also begin to move and behave during this skandha. For example, the simple perception of a travel poster may set in motion a great deal of mental activity. We may begin recalling an old trip or begin fantasizing about a new one. If we are photographers, we may admire the composition of the photo, step closer to it, make an effort to remember it, and so on. All of these behaviors belong to the skandha of mental activity. Just as the skandha of sensation lies at the base of all emotion, so the skandha of activity lies at the base of all of our actions.

The *Agamas* say, "What is the skandha of activity? It is the actions of the body, the actions of speech and the actions of thought; these are the actions of the skandha of activity." The *Agamas* also say, "Action means that which leads to accomplishment and that is why it is called action. And what does it accomplish? It may accomplish good or it may accomplish evil."

The skandha of activity follows the skandha of perception immediately. Intention is present during this skandha, but since it comes so quickly upon the heels of the skandha of perception, it is usually little more than the blind intention of habit, prejudice, and illusion.

THE SKANDHA OF INDIVIDUAL CONSCIOUSNESS

The fifth skandha is individual consciousness (*vijnana-skandha*). It is a product of the first four skandhas and is profoundly conditioned by them. During the skandha of individual consciousness the heaps of data from the other skandhas come to be known in greater depth. This is the skandha wherein complex thought, discrimination, complex judgment and evaluation occur. This is what we normally think of, more or less, as being our "self."

The *Abhidharma-kosha* says, "That which makes distinctions among the many sensory realms and the many things in those realms is called the skandha of individual consciousness. The skandha of individual consciousness functions within the sixth consciousness, or within the sixth consciousness plus one or more of the other five consciousnesses." The *Great Commentary on the Five Skandhas* says, "The skandha of individual consciousness has the nature of discriminating within the realms that condition it. It might an also be called 'mental awareness' because it selects and unites the various elements of awareness."

The Buddha taught the five skandhas primarily to help us understand that the appearance of a self that is generated within this skandha is empty since it is entirely based on the conditions found within the first four skandhas. The *Ekkotarika-agama* explains this point very well when it says, "The Buddha said that the skandha of form is like foam, the skandha of sensation is like a bubble, the skandha of perception is like a wild horse, the skandha of activity is like a banana tree, and thus the skandha of individual consciousness is nothing more than an illusion." The trunk of a banana tree is made of leaves curled together. From the outside, it may look substantial, but if we examine it closely we will find that one leaf pulls away from the next, leaving nothing behind in the end. The trunk looks substantial, but in truth it is "empty." In just this way, our individual consciousness may look substantial to us, but if we peel it apart, we find that there is no self within—it is empty.

HOW TO UNDERSTAND THE FIVE SKANDHAS

Though most of us are not normally aware of the first two skandhas it is possible to become aware of them through meditation and mindfulness practices. While it is easier to begin understanding the five skandhas by thinking of them as being separate and distinct, it is important to realize that any of the last four skandhas can give rise to the skandha of form. Mental activity itself, for example, can generate whole new trains of forms, sensations, and perceptions.

Another important thing to understand about the five skandhas is that our minds move very quickly from one to the next. The five skandhas produce a snow storm of impressions and mentation, upon which rests our unstable conscious world. When we become overly attached to this snow storm or to the consciousness built upon it, we actually generate the karma that fuels the skandhas in the first place.

The *Explanation of Mahayana Terms* says that activation of the skandhas can be understood as being either positive, negative, or neutral. The *Explanation* says that positive activation of the five skandhas can be of three types: activation by a positive form, such as a Buddhist image; activation by skillful means, such as a desire to help someone; and activation within a pure-minded person. The *Explanation* says that the three negative types of activation of the five skandhas result from: simple badness within them, as may have derived from low motives or moodiness; contaminations within them, such as selfishness during an act of kindness; and persistent negativity that is the result of bad karma. The *Explanation* says that the three neutral types of activation are: formal activations that result from the performance of rituals; activations resulting from the practice of a skill; and neutral changes among the skandhas themselves.

HOW TO CONTEMPLATE THE FIVE SKANDHAS

The Buddha taught that all Dharma teachings should be learned in four steps—first we hear them (or read them), next we understand them, then we contemplate them or think about them, and lastly, we get the result of the teaching. Now that we have read and understood the five skandha explanation of the false self, it is time to begin contemplating it. Contemplating the five skandhas appeals to the rational mind, for it allows us to use reason to convince ourselves that the "self" we call our own is, in truth, an illusion. As soon as we begin to understand this illusion for what it is, we will be less likely to cling to it or to perform harmful actions for its supposed "benefit." The result of this is a profound widening of awareness, since the confining energies of pride and anxiety associated with the false self will have become less forceful.

In contemplating, the five skandhas we should be mindful that we begin to generate karma during the skandha of perception. At the same time, it is important to realize that the very forms we see and the sensations that result from them are heavily conditioned by our past actions, by the accumulation of karmic "seeds" or influences that are already stored in our minds. Two people may see exactly the same form, but have very different responses to it because their karma is not the same. Since their karma is different, their sensations and perceptions, and especially their mental activity and consciousness will be very different.

The *Numerical Teachings of Great Ming Dynasty Tripitaka* says that the most important way to understand the five skandhas is to realize that each of them is empty. As we become familiar with the five skandhas, we will find it easier to identify each one and contemplate its emptiness. We can think about them from first to last or from last to first.

If we choose to think of them from last to first, our contemplation will consist of a series of important questions. We begin by asking ourselves what the skandha of individual consciousness is based upon. The answer is the skandha of mental activity. The skandha of mental activity becomes apparent for most of us as soon as we sit down to meditate—thoughts and feelings rise and fall in a jumble that is frenzied, disorganized, and uncontrolled. This is the engine room of the self, the confused and confusing substrate of individual consciousness. Having identified this skandha and appreciated its fundamental emptiness, we can ask ourselves what it is based upon. The answer is the skandha of perception. First the mind seizes one of its impressions (the skandha of perception), then a long train of thought and emotion follows (the skandha of activity). Having appreciated this process, we then ask ourselves what the skandha of perception is based upon. The answer is sensation—of the many forms and feelings passing through our minds, one of them gave rise to either a positive or negative sensation (neutral sensations are usually ignored by the mind). It is this sensation that led to the skandha of perception. If we can appreciate this, then we can ask what the skandha of sensation is based upon. The answer is form—either an outer or inner form. Were it not for this form, none of the other skandhas would have arisen.

If we choose to contemplate from the first skandha to the last, we may choose a form and then carefully watch how our minds process it. We will see that form leads to sensation, then to perception, then to activity, and lastly to individual consciousness—a state of mind deeply colored by the skandhas below it. For example, the form of a wild animal in the woods may give rise to sensations of fear, then a more detailed perception of the animal, followed by the mental activity of deciding how to behave. Each of these skandhas will have a great influence on the individual consciousness that rests upon them. A second example might be the form of a stranger who resembles someone we love. This form will very likely give rise to sensations of pleasure and the perception that this is someone we might enjoy or whom we can trust. If we are introduced to this stranger, our perceptions will probably lead to positive mental activity and agreeable behavior that will of themselves dispose the person to like us. The friendly state of consciousness that develops "on top of" these skandhas will thus largely have arisen from a very basic predisposition that was associated with the form of the person, our first impression of them.

The quotation cited previously from the *Ekkotarika-agama* can also be used as a very fine contemplation. The agama says, "The Buddha said that the skandha of form is like foam, the skandha of sensation is like a bubble, the skandha of perception is like a wild horse, the skandha of activity is like a banana tree, and thus the skandha of individual consciousness is nothing more than an illusion." The skandha of form is like foam in a stream—at any moment scores of forms contend for our attention. The skandha of sensation is like a bubble—suddenly we react to a single bubble within the foam. The skandha of perception is like a wild horse—we can never be sure which way our mind will turn at this point. The skandha of activity is like a banana tree—it consists of many things wrapped together. And thus, the skandha of individual consciousness is empty, an illusion.

THE TWELVE LINKS

The twelve links in the chain of existence (Sanskrit: the twelve *nidanas*) explain the causes and conditions that underlie reincarnation, or the cycle of birth and death. Understanding the twelve links helps us understand where we came from and where we will go when our present lives are over. The Buddha taught that all sentient beings are trapped in a cycle of birth and death that has no beginning and no end. He taught the twelve links to help sentient beings understand this cycle and free themselves from it.

The twelve links are the Buddha's most basic explanation of dependent origination applied to sentient life. In this explanation he describes the causes and conditions that give rise to continuity within one life and from one life to the next. The Buddha taught both that all things are caused and that all things are supported by conditions. By understanding the causes behind our lives, we will come closer to understanding the origin of our lives. By understanding the conditions that underlie our lives, we will come closer to understanding how one life moment is connected to the next, one day to the next, one year to the next, and one life to the next. Though the twelve-links explanation of the cycle of birth and death is part of the Buddha's basic teachings, it is not always easy to fully understand, for it requires us to see life from several different angles at once. Additionally, it asks that we first realize that time has no beginning or end, that nothing stands alone, and that no sentient being possesses an enduring self or soul.

Most explanations of the origin of life require a first cause or discrete beginning. The Buddha said that there is no such beginning. He taught instead that the cycle of birth and death is "beginningless and endless." Though time may have a direction (past to present to future), it does not possess an absolute nature. It is not a "stage" upon which life is enacted, but rather a quality or condition that, like all other conditions, is dependent on other things. Though the phenomenal universe itself may come to an end, the cycle of birth and death will not, for the conditions that underlie this cycle are more basic than the conditions that underlie phenomena.

Ignorance is the first of the twelve links and the source of all suffering in this world. The most basic form of ignorance is failure to understand the connection between cause and effect. Other basic forms of ignorance are not understanding impermanence, not understanding the absence of an absolute "self" in anything, not understanding the significance of our intentions, or the fact that each thing in the universe is dependent on many other things. The *Awakening of Faith in the Mahayana* says, "All defiled causes are ignorance." The *Medallion Sutra on the Bodhisattva Way* says, "Ignorance means not understanding the way things are." All forms of ignorance can be thought of as hindrances or blockages that prevent our seeing the truth. Since ignorance itself has no beginning, it sometimes also is called "beginningless ignorance."

The second of the twelve links is activity or behavior. Due to the first link (ignorance) our behavior often springs from bad intentions, thereby generating karmic results. The Buddha grouped human behavior (and thus karma) into three basic categories—those of body, speech, and mind. The *Flower Garland Sutra* says, "There are two kinds of activity—the continuous generation of karmic causes and the continuous suffering resulting from those causes."

The third of the twelve links is individual consciousness, or "karmic consciousness"—that state of awareness that is brought about as a result of our past actions. This link first appears in any distinct incarnation at the moment the egg cell is fertilized or very shortly thereafter.

The fourth of the twelve links is called "name and form." Name refers to the four skandhas of sensation, perception, activity, and individual consciousness, while form refers to the material body associated with those skandhas. The word name is used in place of the four mental skandhas because this link in the cycle of birth and death begins very soon after an egg cell is fertilized, at a moment when these skandhas are still incipient.

The fifth of the twelve links are the sensory organs—eye, ear, nose, tongue, body, and the nervous and cerebral systems that coordinate these. These organs begin to appear during fetal development.

The sixth of the twelve links is contact. Once functioning sense organs come into contact with their environment, this link has been established.

The seventh link is sensation. Once the mind feels sensation—positive, negative, or neutral—this link has been established.

The eighth link is desire. Once the mind has experienced a sensation, it may either be attracted to it or repelled by it. This attraction or revulsion are both considered to comprise the "desire" of this link.

The ninth link is "clinging" or "attachment." Following the desire of the eighth link comes habituation to our desires or attachment to them. Clinging can be understood in four basic ways: clinging to sensory pleasures, clinging to intellectual habits, clinging to rigid or imperfect moral rules, and clinging to a delusive sense of self.

The tenth link is existence, which means the "existence" of karma. The links just before this one—sensation, desire, and clinging—are the points at which karma is generated, since intention is active during these links. This tenth link describes the karma that has just been generated. The third of the twelve links—karmic consciousness—arises from the karmic seeds that are planted at this point, or the karmic influences generated at this point.

The eleventh link is "birth" or "arising." Due to the seeds planted during the tenth link, new karmic conditions will arise or be born. This link can be thought of as the start of a new life or as the start of new conditions within life.

The last of the twelve links is called "old age and death." The Buddha taught that all things that arise must decline and be extinguished—everything grows old and dies. This link can be thought of as the end of a life or as the end of conditions within a life.

HOW TO UNDERSTAND THE TWELVE LINKS

The twelve links can and should be understood in several ways—from the point of view of several incarnations, from the point of view of a single incarnation, from the point of view of the moment, and as a way of understanding successive existential change from moment to moment or life to life. Since the process being described by the Buddha's explanation of the twelve links is fundamentally both rooted in delusion and empty, it is important not to become attached to it and thus miss its capacity to help us find liberation from what it describes.

From the point of view of several incarnations, the twelve links can be understood in terms of our past, present, and future lives. During our past lives we have behaved out of ignorance (first link) and thus set in motion causes that led to activities (second link) that planted karmic seeds. This stage marks the origin or arising of all that will follow. These two links are known as the "two causes of the past."

Due to the karmic seeds planted in a past life, we harvest the "five fruits" of suffering in this life—karmic consciousness, name and form, the six sense organs, contact, and sensation (the third through the seventh links). These five links are known as the "five fruits (results) of the present."

Having harvested the five fruits mentioned above, we react to them with desire (eighth link) and clinging (ninth link). Our desire and clinging give rise to the existence (tenth link) of more karmic seeds. These three links are known as the "three causes of the present."

The existence of these new karmic seeds leads to our eventual (re)birth (eleventh link) and old age and death (twelfth link). These two links are known as the "two fruits of the future."

In the four paragraphs immediately above, the first two paragraphs—concerning past lives and our present life—are called "one kind of cause and effect," while the last two paragraphs—concerning our present life and future lives—are called "another kind of cause and effect." Together, these two sorts of cause and effect are known as the "two kinds of cause and effect." If we think about them deeply, we will be able to see that the first kind gives rise to the second kind, which then gives rise to the first kind again. The process being described is cyclical, and thus it can be difficult to grasp in a linear fashion. The twelve links can be compared to the hands of a clock that have traveled from 12 AM to 12 PM—though they may be in the same position, the times of day they describe are very different. In the very general ways described by the twelve links, one incarnation resembles another, though the specifics of particular incarnations probably will not resemble each other much at all.

From the point of view of a single incarnation, the twelve links can be understood as smaller cycles that whirl and eddy within the larger cycle described above. Viewed this way, the ignorance of youth gives rise to activity during early adolescence that leads to the sensation of suffering during middle adolescence. In late adolescence, these sensations give rise to desires and the tendency to cling, thus planting more karmic seeds which will sprout during adulthood and beyond. When seen from this point of view, desire (eighth link) is generally considered to become predominant between the ages of sixteen and eighteen and clinging (ninth link) around the age of thirty.

From the point of view of the moment, all of the twelve links can be considered to be present at all times. In a moment we may entertain a greedy thought and act upon it immediately. Another way of understanding the twelve links in the moment is to realize that the causes that we have planted in the past are present in our minds at every moment, as are the general features of the results that will flow from these causes. Much of deluded life is spent reacting ignorantly to results that we ourselves have caused. The Buddha's explanations of the five skandhas and the twelve links, in particular, were designed to help us break free of this destructive cycle.

From the point of view of successive change from moment to moment or life to life, the twelve links can be understood as flowing directly from one link to the next. The Buddha called them "links" because each one is locked to the ones beside it. Ignorance gives rise to activity as surely as birth gives rise to death.

The *Treatise on the Perfection of Truth* says that the first ten links can also be understood as causes, while only the last two links—birth, old age and death—are results. Seen in this way, the first ten links are the general causes generated in one life that give rise to the next life.

Tiantai Buddhists say that there are four ways to understand the twelve links—as hidden, as interconnected, as unique to each individual, and as "complete." As *hidden* links, they are seen as factors that affect our lives without our understanding. As *interconnected* links, they are seen as flowing from one to the next, as a whole that is influenced by all of its parts, and as being connected to everything else in the world. As *unique to each individual*, they are seen as being general explanations whose fullness is realized only when applied to particular lives. Lastly, as *complete*, the twelve links are equated with Buddha nature itself, for in this way of looking at existence, all things are Buddha nature. This view is also known as the "middle view," which is so named because it encompasses a unity of ultimate and relative truths (see chapter 12 for more on this). Tiantai contemplations of the twelve links are primarily aimed at deconstructing the "self" or "self views;" i.e. that the self has intrinsic being, that it is permanent, or that it is profitable to cling to its wants. If these views are overcome, then the ultimate source of all karma has been overcome.

The *Flower Garland Sutra* says, "Ignorance gives rise to all activity and maintains its continuation by enabling it. Activity gives rise to individual consciousness and maintains its continuation by enabling it. Individual consciousness gives rise to name and form and maintains their continuation by enabling them. This same general process pertains to all of the rest of the twelve links from birth to old age, death, and suffering. This process maintains the continuation of death by enabling it. If ignorance is extinguished, then activity will be extinguished, as will all of the other twelve links including birth, old age, death, and suffering. If the cause is extinguished, then the effect will also be extinguished."

HOW TO CONTEMPLATE THE TWELVE LINKS

Contemplating the twelve links helps us understand how our thoughts and actions give rise to the conditions that prevail in our lives. This understanding then helps us break the "chain" that the twelve links describe and free ourselves from the cycle of birth and death. When the individual consciousness that is conditioned by karmic fruits begins to understand its own limitations and their causes, it is in position to open itself to the enlightened Buddha mind that underlies it.

The *Agamas* say that the Buddha himself achieved enlightenment by long contemplation of the twelve links and that since he had compassion for sentient beings "who did not understand the twelve links and thus remained trapped in the endless cycle of birth and death, and who were thoroughly deluded and did not comprehend the sources of their behavior or how one life was connected to another," used skillful means to teach them how to liberate themselves from their suffering.

The most basic way to contemplate the twelve links is to examine them in order. First we contemplate what the Buddha meant by ignorance (first link), then we contemplate how ignorance gives rise to behavior (second link), and then how this behavior gives rise to our individual "consciousness" or state of mind (third link). For example, if we are ignorant and act in anger, then we will produce, among other things, a bruised state of mind that is mainly bent on justifying whatever it has done. This consciousness then colors the five skandhas and affects the health of the body. These states then alter our perceptions of the world and influence the sensations that we derive from it. These sensations then give rise to desire and clinging and the generation of more karma. This karma then gives rise to new situations which ultimately grow old and die. This basic contemplation can be done either from the point of view of one life, several lives, the moment, a day, or a mixture of all of these.

The second important way to contemplate the twelve links is to think of them in reverse order. In this contemplation we ask ourselves a series of questions and try to answer them. For example, we might start by asking why is there death and answer that there is death because there is old age. If we ask why there is old age, we might answer by saying that it arises because there was birth. Then where does birth come from? It is a product of karma. Then where did the karma come from? It came from clinging to deluded views. And where did these come from? From our desires and emotions. And where did these come from? From our sensations. And where did these come from? From the fact that we have had contact with the world. And what underlies that contact? The presence of sense organs. And where did the sense organs come from? From the five skandhas and the existence of the body. And where did these come from? From the existence of our "mind stream" or "karmic consciousness." And where did these come from? From our previous actions. And what characterized these? Our ignorance.

A third way of contemplating the twelve links is to consider that the existence (tenth link) of karma is the foundation of individual consciousness (third link). This ignorant (first link) consciousness then gives rise to activity (second link) and the experience of being a living entity. Due to its ignorance (first link), this living entity seeks satisfaction among the subjective "objects" of its own greed, anger, and ignorance. As it becomes accustomed to living in this way, it inevitably causes itself to suffer. This cycle can be broken by understanding the depth of our ignorance and taking steps to stop generating the karma that fuels it. In this contemplation, we might imagine the twelve links as a more or less balled up chain, rather than a strictly circular one.

Last, we can contemplate the twelve links by thinking about how ignorance (first link) gives rise to activity (second link), which then gives rise to individual consciousness (third link). This consciousness, in turn, affects its own thought processes (the five skandhas) and body (fourth link). These affected agents then influence the sense organs (fifth link), which then influence whatever contact (sixth link) they make with the world and the sensations (seventh link) that are derived from this contact. These sensations then condition the desires (eighth link) and fixations (ninth link) that appear. These fixations then lead to the existence of karma (tenth link) and the birth (eleventh link), old age, and death (twelfth link) of whatever events have arisen due to the foregoing process.

Whenever we contemplate the twelve links, we should be mindful of the four noble truths, for the purpose of these contemplations is to free ourselves from suffering.

CONCLUSION

The cycle described by the twelve links can be compared to a river that sweeps us downstream or to a prison that keeps us confined to a narrow and unsatisfying choice of options. Buddhist sutras sometimes say that this prison is guarded by the formidable demons of greed, anger, ignorance, pride, and sloth. To escape from this prison, we must overcome each of these guards.

The twelve links can also be compared to a fruit tree. Once the fruit of a tree has fallen to the ground and its seed has taken root, a shoot will grow and gradually turn into a second tree. This tree in turn will eventually bloom and produce another fruit which will fall to the ground and give rise to a third tree. Though each tree is different from the others, they have been produced from the same basic conditions. Sentient beings give rise to one life after another in a process that very much resembles the process that gives rise to one fruit tree after another.

The twelve links sometimes are referred to by other names. The *Sutra on the Verse of Five Sufferings* calls them the "twelve walls" because they trap sentient beings. The *Ekkotarika Agama* calls them the "twelve successions" since one follows after the other. Other texts call them the "twelve wheels" since, left to themselves, they will turn without ceasing.

The *Madhyama-agama* says:

> If we can understand the suffering that is caused by being trapped in the cycle of the twelve links and if we have faith (in the Dharma), then our faith will give rise to correct contemplation (of this cycle). In time, our contemplations will give rise to right thought and wisdom and these will aid us in the deepest parts of our minds—they will help us uphold the precepts, be without regret, joyful and glad, stable, happy, able to meditate, and able to see the truth. Further, they will help us shrink from the causes of suffering, be without desire, and break the bonds of delusion. Ultimately they will help us attain nirvana.

SAMADHI

The Sanskrit word *samadhi* literally means "concentration" in English. Often it is translated as "meditation" or "concentration," or simply left untranslated. In most contexts, these renderings work very well, but if we want to delve more deeply into our samadhi states and understand how these states can be used to further our practice of Buddhism, it is crucial that we first look more deeply into the meaning of the word samadhi.

There are two basic kinds of samadhi: ordinary samadhi and the cultivated samadhi states that arise from Buddhist meditation practices. Ordinary samadhi refers to all states of the ordinary deluded mind. Delusion itself is a kind of samadhi state. Ordinary samadhi states can be defined as simply "the state of paying attention to something" or "the state of concentrating on something." These states might be compared to what we call "trances" in English, or "fixations." They are generated by karma and arise out of ignorance. When we are seduced by them, we invariably light one or more of the three fires of greed, anger, or ignorance. One of the deepest ordinary samadhi states is the profound trance induced by believing in a permanent self. Less deep ordinary samadhi states might involve fixations on things or people that we passionately desire, zealous political or intellectual convictions, persistent anger, or an intransigent inability to forgive. Shallow samadhi states might include such things as watching TV, inattentively reading a book, eating a meal, talking with a friend, playing sports, and so on. The important thing to understand about these states is that they indicate a function of the mind—its ability to concentrate or fix its attention on something.

The second kind of samadhi involves Buddhist meditation and mindfulness practices. These practices are designed to show us how to use our ability to concentrate to arrive at even deeper and more wholesome states of samadhi. Once we have begun to understand how our minds concentrate and why they pay attention to the things they do, we will be in an excellent position to start using the deep samadhi states generated by Buddhist meditation to transform awareness itself.

Before we begin our discussion of Buddhist samadhi states, let us look more deeply at the word samadhi itself. Samadhi is a compound word made up of three Sanskrit words—*sam*, *a*, and *dhi*. *Sam* means "together," *a* means "toward," and *dhi* means "to put" or "to place." When the contents of our minds are "put together," we have attention or concentration. Another interpretation of this etymology is that samadhi more literally means "to establish" or "make firm." As we continue our discussion, it is important to remember that the basic meaning of samadhi denotes a spectrum that grades from very ordinary samadhi states all the way to the profound states of meditation.

When Buddhists use the word samadhi, they generally are referring to the higher samadhi states produced by Buddhist meditation practices. In these states, the mind is still "concentrated," as it were, but it is no longer fixated or concentrated on a single point. Rather, its "concentration" has become so deep and vast it transcends the very possibility of fixating on any phenomenal thing. In these states, the subject and object of meditation merge into a samadhi characterized by even-mindedness, tranquility, absence of self, and disentanglement from all delusive mental and emotional constructs. This state is sometimes described as "the mind is one with its nature and realm." This means that the mind has rediscovered the deep level of reality that underlies both itself and the world around it. If we can understand how the meaning of the basic word "concentration" has been expanded to include this profound state, we should also be able to appreciate how this profound state is quite different from what we normally think of as concentration. Concentration is the beginning, mindfulness and deep states of meditation are the middle, enlightenment is the end.

Though samadhi states are used on the path to enlightenment, they are not the same as enlightenment. Buddhist meditation practices were designed to help us become wise, and to help us understand and control our minds as we disentangle ourselves from the cycle of birth and death, but they were not designed to be an end in themselves. To cling to samadhi states is to contract the "illness of Chan," a trance-like torpor that can result from misunderstanding the deep purpose of Buddhist meditation practices.

SAMADHI AND LAKSHANA

To delve even more deeply into the meaning of the word samadhi, we should look briefly at another basic word used in virtually all Buddhist texts to describe the mind. This word is *lakshana*. It denotes all elements of the deluded mind. The five skandhas consist solely of lakshana—all forms are lakshana, all sensations are lakshana, all perceptions are lakshana, all trains of mental activity are made up of lakshana, and all of the "contents" of deluded awareness are lakshana. All of the "contents" of the twelve links are also lakshana. In the *Diamond Sutra* the Buddha says, "If you can see that all lakshana are delusive, you will see the Tathagata." Tathagata is one of the ten names of the Buddha. In this context it means the enlightened Buddha mind.

The word *lakshana* is often translated as "sign," "mark," or "characteristic" in English. In most contexts, these translations work well enough, but if we want to see very deeply into the Buddha's message, we must broaden our understanding of the word lakshana beyond these English translations. If ordinary samadhi states are basically what our minds do when they pay attention, lakshana are the objects of that ordinary attention. Lakshana can be sights, sounds, dreams, thoughts, memories, emotions, sensations, or anything else that can be a focal point of the deluded, or ordinary, mind. They can also be understood as the units, the elements, or the manifestations of our karma. Buddhist meditation practices are designed to help us see through all lakshana and disentangle ourselves from them.

When we study samadhi states, then, we are doing two things at once. First, we engage in an inquiry into our attention or concentration. And second, we disentangle ourselves from the many lakshana that constantly swirl through our minds. Once we have begun to see through lakshana and not fixate on them or be led by them, we will have begun to enter into the deep states of Buddhist meditation called the "eight samadhis."

Before we discuss the eight samadhis, it should be mentioned that Buddhist meditation practices cannot be properly undertaken in isolation from the rest of the Buddha's teachings. Meditation is only one aspect of the three basic elements of all Buddhist practice. These three elements are usually called the "three trainings." They are morality, meditation, and wisdom. Morality is the foundation of Buddhist practice. Mediation is built upon this foundation. Then with these two bases securely in place, we can begin to make real progress toward becoming wise. To omit any one of these basic aspects of the Buddha's teachings is to severely hinder them all. If we are living a moral life, meditation will be much easier, for when we treat others well, we avoid all of the storms and conflicts that make meditation all but impossible. Additionally, we stop generating the negative karma that can make the practice of Buddhism so difficult. On top of all of this, we will gain a clarity and peace of mind that allows us to absorb the Buddha's wisdom teachings much more easily. First we hear, then we understand, then we practice, and then we get the result. When the Buddha's teachings are learned and practiced correctly, the results we attain are truly wondrous.

THE EIGHT SAMADHIS

Just as our understanding of English Buddhist terms changes as we learn more about Buddhism, so our understanding of Sanskrit terms will change as we progress in our practice. The technical meaning of *samadhi* is the "four meditative states of the formless realm." In practice, as we have seen, this word has come to be used for all states of concentration, including the "four meditative states of the form realm," the technical word for which is *dhyana* (absorption). The four dhyanas plus the four samadhis are commonly called simply the "eight samadhis."

The first four samadhi states, or dhyanas, are also called "tranquil wisdom" in Chinese. Since these states occur within the form realm, they are not as deep as the second group of four samadhi states, which occur within the formless realm. This saha world (the world of delusion) consists of three realms—the form realm, the formless realm, and the realm of desire (see chapter 3 for more on the three realms). Our ordinary minds operate almost exclusively within the desire realm. As we progress in our practice of meditation, we will begin to experience the realms of form and formlessness. Basically, the form realm is characterized by having forms but being devoid of desire, while the formless realm has neither forms nor desire. We can see from this explanation why the samadhi states themselves are not considered to be fully enlightened states, for not one of the eight samadhis transcends all three of these realms. The samadhi states are tools that we use to understand the deep levels of sentient life. Coupled with the Buddha's other teachings, these tools will help us attain complete, unsurpassed enlightenment, or Buddhahood.

I will discuss each of the eight samadhi states below:

The Four Samadhis of the Form Realm. The first samadhi state is characterized by an absence of desire and a complete quieting of the senses of smell and taste. Thought and the other senses remain active and are characterized by the general tendency to want to find the truth and the specific act of searching within themselves for this truth. This state is further characterized by feelings of joy and fulfillment, for the mind, at least briefly, has disentangled itself from all desire.

The second samadhi state, which follows the first, is characterized by the complete quieting of the senses of sight, hearing, and touch, in addition to the senses of smell and taste, which were quieted in the first samadhi state. The joy of this state is greater than that of the first samadhi because the mind's tendency to search for truth has also been quieted. This state deepens our faith in the teachings because it allows us to experience levels of truth that lie beneath both words and the senses. This state is sometimes called "inner even-mindedness and clarity," for it is further marked by a brilliant inner transparency that replaces the comparative darkness of the first samadhi state.

The third samadhi state is characterized by a complete quieting of all of the senses except thought, which becomes exceptionally pure. The mind is unattached and does not cling even to the joys inherent in this state. This samadhi is sometimes called the "first joy of this world" since the joy that characterizes it is not clung to and thus flows unimpeded throughout the body and mind.

The fourth samadhi state is characterized by exceptional tranquility and clarity. Thoughts do not arise, the breath stops, and the mind is like a body of water upon which there are no waves.

The Four Samadhis of the Formless Realm. The fifth samadhi state is the first samadhi of the formless realm. In this state, the mind is absorbed in emptiness and has transcended all three kinds of form discussed in the section on the skandha of form (see chapter 4). One feels like a soaring bird that has just been released from a cage.

The sixth samadhi state is characterized by an exceptionally pure and clear awareness that is not bound by any of the mundane constraints that normally condition our minds. There remains only a deeply tranquil awareness of past, present, and future states of individual consciousness.

The seventh samadhi state is characterized by its transcendence of both emptiness and the pure individual consciousness of the sixth samadhi state. No mental dharmas arise in this state.

The eighth samadhi state transcends emptiness, thought, individual consciousness, location, and anything that can be associated with any of these.

Samadhi states are normally experienced in seated meditation. Generally speaking, most people experience the first samadhi state and deeply enjoy it until they begin to realize that more is available to them. This leads them to the second samadhi state. This general progression continues from one samadhi state to the next—first we enjoy the state and learn from it, then we begin to realize that we can go still deeper. Though the samadhi states are exceptionally pleasant, they should not be considered an end in themselves, for the fundamental purpose of all Buddhist meditation practice is to help us understand our minds and free them from their many unwholesome fixations

The *Sutra on the Explication of Mysteries* says, "If a good man or a good woman should enter these samadhi states, his or her mind will not be restless and thus able to understand all manner of physical and mental activity. When one enters samadhi, one is able to think about and analyze all kinds of things without making mistakes."

HOW TO USE THE SAMADHI STATES

Deeply understood, samadhi states are themselves a form of wisdom. At the same time, these states are like microscopes that allow us to see very deeply into the workings of our minds. When we are familiar with even the most basic samadhi states, we will be much better able to behave correctly and to learn more about ourselves. With more practice, we will find that we can actually use the vantage of the samadhi states to perceive the very "roots" of our selfish urges and attachments and pull them out for good. This completely painless operation requires nothing more than a single thought activated at the right time and directed toward the right "root." In just a moment, complex fixations replete with numerous lakshana and desires can be uprooted and removed forever from the mind stream. This is possible because experience with the samadhi states allows us to grip these roots at their points of origin. When Buddhist texts say that we must strive to "cut" our unwholesome roots or "uproot" our harmful fixations, they are basically describing this process.

If we understand how our minds fixate and what is meant by "delusive lakshana," our experience with samadhi states will allow us to radically change the way we approach our cognitive functions. In the light of the Buddha's other teachings, we will find that the deepened consciousness discovered in samadhi states is one of the most valuable aids we have to cure our minds of the three diseases of greed, anger, and ignorance.

The samadhi states should be thought of as tools. When we have finished using these tools, we will not fly off to some other world, but find instead that we are in this world more completely than we ever have been before. The world will be the same, but our awareness of it will be deepened by a factor that "cannot even be suggested by metaphors," as many sutras say.

Some things to guard against while learning the eight samadhis are pride, laziness, irritability, confusion, and fear. Pride can block our progress if we become conceited about having reached a certain stage ahead of other people. If the samadhi states are not properly understood, they can sometimes engender laziness or carelessness in other parts of our lives. This can be corrected by reflecting on the purpose of meditation. Irritability can sometimes result from shallow meditative states. Watch irritability if it does appear, for it can be rather amusing—here we are seeking deep peace and this is what happens. This state just shows that our minds are not yet well trained and need more time to adjust to stillness. Confusion and fear may briefly appear in meditative states, since the mind is no longer depending upon its normal dose of sensory input, but these states rarely last very long, if they appear at all. Of course, each of the defilements mentioned above, and many others, may also prevent us from meditating at all. The Buddha taught meditation and used it in his own quest for enlightenment. This fact alone should alert us to the importance of exploring the samadhi states.

The eight samadhis are normally learned in seated meditation, and yet when we begin to meditate, most of us discover that we cannot control our minds. The tumultuous mental activity of the fourth skandha so dominates our awareness that we hardly know what to do with ourselves. Buddhist masters have given us many techniques to help us bring tranquility to our minds. Foremost among them is the technique of "counting the breath." With this technique we "watch" our breath by mentally counting ten breaths at a time while focusing on the passage of air through the nose. We count either our inhalations or exhalations. Once we have counted ten of them, we stop and allow our minds to rest. If the mind still feels turbulent, we count another set of ten breaths. We can repeat this technique as many times as we like. The advantage of breath counting lies in its simplicity. By giving our minds a little something to do, we guide them toward deeper states of tranquility. As we count our breaths, it is important not to try to control them or the thoughts that may be swirling in our minds. Just breathe naturally, relax, and let the technique do the rest. This is the most basic of all Buddhist meditation techniques, and very likely, the most effective. It is used by both beginning and advanced meditators. After we have counted our breath a few times and feel relaxed, we begin to "watch the breath" by slightly paying attention to it as it passes through the nose.

Other things to be mindful of when meditating are the place we meditate, our posture, the time of day, and our attitude. A quiet place is the best place to start practicing meditation, but if one is not available, we can begin anyway. Sometimes the noises of the world can even be an aid to our practice. Many Buddhists have a small altar in their homes and like to meditate in front of that. It is nice to have a place like this in our homes dedicated to meditation, but not necessary. In fact, it is a very good idea to move your seat to a new location from time to time. Meditation is an "internal" practice, and thus should not be dependent on external surroundings. Group meditations, if available in your area, are also extremely helpful, for the group helps us with our discipline and gives us a chance to learn from, and help, others.

The best seated meditation posture is the "full lotus" position, in which we sit cross-legged with the feet resting on the thighs. Many people find this posture difficult and use the "half-lotus" position instead. In the half-lotus we are still cross-legged, but only one foot is placed on top of the thigh (the left on top of the right, say), while the other is placed beneath the thigh (the right beneath the left). If even this position is uncomfortable, a chair, a stool, or the edge of a bed can be used. The back should be straight and comfortable, the chin level, the eyes closed or slightly open, and the breathing natural.

Most people meditate in the morning and evening, though we can do it at any time of day. It is usually better not to meditate soon after eating or when we are sleepy. Our attitude toward meditation should be relaxed, respectful, patient, and determined enough to keep at it. The fruits of meditation generally take some time to fully ripen, so we need to be disciplined in our practice. The times when we least feel like meditating are often the times that we get the most out of it.

Meditation practice deepens as the years go by. If we are resolute and faithful to it, we will eventually discover all of the eight samadhi states described above. The Buddhadharma has been passed down to us in words and is mostly conveyed in words, but the samadhi states are completely beyond words. If we want to deepen our understanding of the Buddha's teachings, we must take the time to explore these wonderful states of mind and use them to understand and transform ourselves. Dharma teachings conveyed in words are like the surface conditions of a deep body of water— they indicate where to dive and tell us roughly what to do once we have dived, but we cannot possibly realize what they really mean unless we ourselves actually enter into these magnificent non-verbal realms.

The *Essays on Samantha Vipassana* says, "How should we learn to meditate? The Buddha said that learning to meditate is like learning archery— first we aim at a large target, then at a smaller one. First we learn simply to hit the target, then we learn to refine our skills. First we aim at a pole, then at a feather, then at a single part of a feather… Similarly, when we learn how to meditate, first we learn the joy of meditation, then we learn how to access our deep minds. After we have learned how to access our deep minds, we learn how to be compassionate. After we have learned how to be compassionate, we learn how to attain the four boundless states of mind."

PRAJNA

The Sanskrit word *prajna* means "wisdom," but is often left untranslated in Buddhist texts because the wisdom referred to by this word is quite different from what we normally mean when we speak about wisdom or say that someone is wise. Buddhist wisdom, or prajna, stands for much more than an accumulation of facts, life experience, or insights into human behavior. The *Flower Garland Sutra* says, "Prajna is the mother of all Buddhas." The *Treatise on the Perfection of Great Wisdom* says, "Prajna is the true characteristic (lakshana) of all dharmas and it cannot be damaged or destroyed."

Prajna is the third element of the three trainings (morality, meditation, and wisdom) upon which all Buddhist practice rests. In this respect, prajna is both a means and an end. It is both that which guides us to the truth and that which is the truth itself. Prajna is also the sixth of the six paramitas (generosity, morality, patience, diligence, concentration, and wisdom) and the most important of them all, for without wisdom, the other paramitas may be practiced incorrectly and sometimes cause more harm than good.

Generally speaking, the word prajna is used in two basic ways in Buddhist texts—to describe all Buddhist practice or to describe the attainment of the highest understanding of Buddhist practice. Underlying this slight mixing of meanings is the very deep idea that our basic natures already are wise. When we listen to them and allow them to guide us, we are being guided by prajna. When we reach our goal, we will have found in fact something that was already there. Tiantai Buddhist practice refers to this process when it says "when our minds are clear, we will see our true nature." When we truly understand who we are, we will understand that we already are enlightened and that the Buddha mind can be seen in everything.

BASIC PRAJNA

The most basic meaning of prajna is "all of the teachings of the Buddha," for all of them are capable of leading us to the truth. More commonly, however, prajna refers to the Buddha's "wisdom teachings," which primarily include the topics of emptiness, dependent origination, no-self, impermanence, and the omnipresence of nirvana. The *Great Prajna Sutra* says, "When we realize these truths, we will escape from the cycle of birth and death."

The Buddha's prajna teachings were primarily designed to help us understand, and thus overcome, the delusion of believing that we have an absolute, separate self. This erroneous belief is the principal source of all suffering. As this belief crumbles, new vistas within the mind appear. These vistas are the luminous realm of prajna. We do not leave this world when we become wise. Rather, we see this world with new eyes.

The *Treatise on the Perfection of Great Wisdom* says, "Prajna is supreme, unsurpassable, incomparable, and without equal. There is nothing better than prajna."

Buddhist texts refer to three levels of prajna—the prajna of skillful means, the prajna of contemplation, and the prajna of the "true characteristic," or enlightenment itself.

The first level—the prajna of skillful means—refers to how we learn, what we learn, and when we learn it. If our teachers are skillful, they will present Dharma ideas in a rational order that suits our capacity to understand them. If we as students are skillful, we will realize that our own efforts are every bit as important as the skill of our teachers, for if we rely solely on what others present to us, we may impede our understanding as no teaching technique can ever be perfect. Our teachers may be monks or nuns, friends, lay Dharma teachers, academics, books, recordings, or life itself. Our original teacher, of course, is Shakyamuni Buddha. If we listen attentively to what he said, through whichever means it may come to us, we will have fulfilled this first level of prajna.

The second level—the prajna of contemplation—refers to what we do with Dharma teachings once we have received them. If we hear them and then forget what was taught, it will be as if we had never heard them at all. Once we have come into contact with a new teaching, we should strive to fully understand it by contemplating its meaning. During our contemplations, we might ask ourselves how this part of the Dharma relates to other parts of the Dharma, how it relates to our lives, and how we are to use it to become wise. When our contemplations lead to deepened practice of the Dharma , we can be sure that we are fulfilling this second level of prajna.

The third level—the prajna of the "true characteristic"—refers to deep realization of the truth. This level is something that most of us only glimpse from time to time. This level is indicated by words, but is essentially a non-verbal state of complete awareness. Ultimately, it is the Buddha mind, the enlightened mind itself. When Master Huineng said that "all prajna arises from our basic nature," he was indicating that this third, and deepest, level of prajna already lies within us.

Since this level of awareness is so deep, it is not possible to grasp it with words. It is something that is discovered after years of Buddhist practice. The *Treatise on the Perfection of Great Wisdom* says, "Prajna is not something that can be apprehended within the realm of the skandhas. It is neither a conditioned nor an unconditioned dharma, neither a thought nor a non-thought. It can neither be grasped nor let go of. It neither arises nor is extinguished. When it appears, it cannot be expressed in words. When we reach it, we cannot take hold of it. It is like a fire that cannot be touched from any angle, for if we try to touch it, we will only burn our hands. Prajna is like that—it cannot be touched with words, for whenever we try, we succeed only in burning ourselves with false views."

TURNING KNOWLEDGE INTO WISDOM

"Turning knowledge into wisdom" is a phrase used by Mind Only Buddhists, who say that mind—the individual mind or the Buddha mind, depending on our point of view—underlies everything (see chapter 12 for more on Mind Only Buddhism). Two people can be in roughly the same situation, but if one of them accepts his conditions and works to make them better, he will always be more successful than the one who causes conflict and reacts with anger. One person understands how to "turn knowledge into wisdom," while the other does not.

The minds of sentient beings are affected by two types of information: the conditioned dharmas that impinge upon the sense organs, and the unconditioned dharmas that are aspects of the enlightened Buddha mind. Conditioned dharmas are all phenomenal things that are subject to change, while unconditioned dharmas provide a rough description of the enlightened state. The unconditioned dharmas are: timelessness, absence of delusion, agelessness, deathlessness, purity, universality, motionlessness, and joy.

The five sense organs of sight, hearing, taste, smell, and touch provide us with information that pertains exclusively to the phenomenal world, which is made up entirely of conditioned dharmas. The human mind—the sixth "sense" organ in Buddhism—is also largely conditioned by these same dharmas. However, it is possible for the mind to receive information concerning the unconditioned dharmas. When this latter sort of information influences our thought processes, we have begun to "turn knowledge into wisdom." This process begins when we realize that what we see is dependent on the conditions that prevail within our minds. If we have a bad attitude, we will see a gloomy world, while if we are given to more positive thoughts, the world we see will not look so disturbing. As Mind Only Buddhists say, "Good and bad arise solely in the mind."

The five most basic sense organs provide us with information, while the mind provides us with analyses, abstractions, and concepts built upon that information. With these tools, the mind is then capable of generating three kinds of thought and behavior—good, bad, and neutral. Bad thoughts and behaviors are those that harm others, that cling to a false sense of self, or are inspired by greed, anger, or ignorance. Good behaviors are those that help others, that tend toward the truth, or are inspired by generosity, compassion, or wisdom. Both of these groups of thought and behavior produce karmic seeds. "Turning knowledge into wisdom" is largely concerned with using the second group of behaviors to understand and overcome the first. It seeks to make the karma-generating mind pure, contemplative, and wise.

After we have made some progress in our study of Buddhism, Mind Only Buddhists say that we are ready to actualize, or fully realize, three important insights into the nature of reality. Each of these insights can be attained only after we have begun to "turn knowledge into wisdom."

The first insight is that of "completeness" or "wholeness." This insight or state of mind results from the wholesome integration of all mental functions. When our minds are without selfish, distracting, or biased thoughts, we will be able to see with the "wisdom eye" and contemplate the world as it really is.

The second insight or state of mind is "brightness" or "enlightenment." It results from the purification of all mental functions. In this state of mind, nothing is concealed or hidden. The world we see is as if reflected in a flawless mirror. Nothing is added and nothing is taken away.

The third insight is "purity." In this state, the mind has no selfish or defiled tendencies whatever. This state of purity allows us to comprehend reality with perfect impartiality.

The "world" or "reality" mentioned in these descriptions is a "pure" and "enlightened" integration (i.e. "wholeness") of the outer and the inner, the objective and the subjective. Successful attainment of these states of mind is metaphorically compared to a full autumn moon, for in its roundness (wholeness), brightness, and purity, the moon reflects perfectly the light of the sun, which is the Buddha mind itself.

When the above insights are applied to the world we live in they correspond to the three attainments. The insight of wholeness is marked by understanding both the universal and individual characteristics of all phenomena. The universal characteristics are the three Dharma seals of impermanence, no-self, and nirvana, which are aspects of all conditioned dharmas. Individual characteristics are all characteristics that demark individual dharmas or phenomena—the liquid qualities of water, for example, the motion of the wind, the solidity of the earth, or the transforming power of fire. In addition to these, all of the many qualities that distinguish this thing from that, or this person from that one, are also individual characteristics. This insight marks fulfillment, or near fulfillment, of the wisdom aspect of the three trainings.

The insight of brightness or enlightenment refers to the attainment of deep samadhi states and the non-verbal comprehension of reality that they afford us. This insight marks fulfillment, or near fulfillment, of the meditation (samadhi) aspect of the three trainings.

The insight of purity allows us to understand other sentient beings as they really are and thus to be of real help to them, since we are beyond making prejudicial judgments based on notions of what will benefit us. This insight marks fulfillment, or near fulfillment, of the morality aspect of the three trainings.

Once we have attained these insights, or begun to attain them, we will see the world differently than we did before. From the vantage of these insights, we will be further able to turn even more "knowledge into wisdom." A first result will be that we will understand the essential equality of all sentient beings and all conditioned dharmas. This will allow us to treat others with deep compassion and to have patience in all situations. A second result is that we will begin generating less karma. When our thoughts and behavior do not arise out of a murky mind stream, they will have much less karmic effect. Our purified intentions will not create conditions that will come back to haunt us later.

WHEN OUR MINDS ARE CLEAR, WE WILL SEE OUR TRUE NATURE

This Tiantai phrase indicates a way of thinking about the mind that will help us attain greater states of wisdom or prajna. It means that when we fully understand our own minds, we will be capable of seeing our deep Buddha nature. It is based on the idea that the Buddha's teachings must be internalized to be fully understood. If we seek outside of ourselves for enlightenment, we will never find it. But if we seek inside ourselves, we will, for once we understand our own minds, we will be capable of drawing out their deepest potential. The *Lotus Sutra* touches on this when it says, "The Dharma is so high it can be difficult for people to understand. However, if we contemplate our minds, it is easy to understand, for the mind, the Buddha, and sentient beings are all fundamentally the same." This way of approaching the Dharma keeps us from spending too much time looking outside of ourselves for truths that already lie within us.

There are several ideas that can guide us in discovering our Buddha nature through understanding our minds.

The first is "it is both large and small." This means that sometimes we will glimpse the Buddha mind as an overwhelming immensity that pervades all things and sometimes we will see it in the tiniest of details. As we recognize both the "largeness" and "smallness" of this enlightened mind, we will surely also see that our own minds are part of this great whole. This awareness stimulates our self-respect, as it reminds us that the ultimate goal of Buddhism is always right here, right now, and never far from us.

The second idea is "it exists both in suffering and in joy." This reminds us that the enlightened mind is not separate from this world but part of it. No matter what our conditions, enlightened consciousness is available to us within them. This awareness teaches us not to shirk our duties or to fear adversity, for if we truly understand the Buddha's teachings, we will recognize that the way is always with us and that nothing can take it from us.

The third idea is "it is both in front of us and behind us." This means that the enlightened mind lies in all directions. No matter where we go, it will be there.

These three ideas can help us keep the deep truths of Buddhism foremost in our minds. If we are feeling lost or confused, they can help us return to the core of our practice. If we become entranced by a single aspect of the Dharma and begin to cling to it, they remind us that the Dharma is everywhere and that to cling to a single part of it is to reduce the whole.

There are three other important ideas that are often associated with the phrase "when our minds are clear, we will see our true nature." I will briefly discuss them below.

The first is: "transcend all relative thoughts." The ordinary human mind spends most of its time comparing, categorizing, and judging data. Each of these activities depends on relativistic thinking patterns. Each of them depends on our examining impermanent phenomena on the basis of transitory distinctions. The deep nature that is revealed when we truly understand our minds is non-relativistic—it is beyond all duality. It is beyond the phenomenal distinctions of hot and cold, up and down, male and female, good and bad, life and death, and so on.

The second is: "give rise to a mind that is not based on anything." This phrase comes from the *Diamond Sutra*, a record of one of the Buddha's most important prajna teachings. The phrase means that our practice of the Dharma must be free of dogmatism, rigid beliefs, self-clinging, and externalism. All clinging to delusion must stop if we are to see our deep natures. The truths indicated by the Dharma are within our "natures"; however, as long as we fail to be "clear about our minds" and how they tend to cling again and again to delusive mental constructs, we will not succeed in "seeing our natures."

The third is: "remain immobile like this," or "remain immobile like the Tathagata." Immobility is a quality of the enlightened mind. It means that enlightenment is changeless, imperturbable, and deeply grounded in reality. Since it is beyond all relative distinctions, it cannot be "moved." When we glimpse these qualities within our own minds, we are glimpsing the Buddha just as surely as when we glimpse boundless compassion or patience. This quality can be most easily discovered by exploring the samadhi states discussed in chapter 6.

The word prajna means "wisdom" in English, but the wisdom referred to is so profound it cannot be strictly defined. If we try to grasp it, we will lose hold of it. Buddhist wisdom is based upon all of the teachings of the Buddha—his moral teachings, which stress compassion; his teachings on the samadhi states, which stress non-verbal attunement with reality; and his teachings on prajna, which repeatedly counsel us not to cling to single points of view or biased interpretations of the truth. Properly understood and carefully studied, these teachings will gradually show us how to overcome all difficulties until we have "cleared our minds" enough to be able to "see our true nature."

The *Great Prajna Sutra* says, "Like the earth that brings forth all manner of good things, profound prajna brings forth all manner of goodness and virtue. Like water that nourishes plants and trees and brings forth their flowers and fruits, profound prajna nourishes even-minded practice and brings forth good methods that result in deep wisdom and the attainment of the fruits of the Dharma. Prajna benefits and brings joy to all sentient beings."

THE FOUR BOUNDLESS STATES OF MIND

M any Dharma teachings help us overcome the delusion of selfhood, but as we begin making progress in this area, we may wonder what is next. As the separate self begins to crumble, we will want to know what replaces it? If I am not that, then what am I? The four boundless states of mind, which describe four aspects of the enlightened mind, are a good way to begin answering this question. As we make progress unraveling the illusion of selfhood and disentangling ourselves from its many strands of greed, pride, anger, laziness, and ignorance, we will discover a lightness of being and a state of joy and clarity that are truly wondrous. More often than not immense feelings of compassion and tolerance also appear around this time. These feelings, or states of mind, are the beginning of bodhicitta, the "bodhi mind."

BODHICITTA

The word *bodhi* means "enlightened." It comes from the same root that gives us the words *Buddha*, "enlightened one," and *bodhisattva*, "enlightened sentient being." *Citta* means "mind." The word *bodhicitta* describes a state of mind that is awake to the unity of itself with all things and clearly understands the path to enlightenment. Bodhicitta is sometimes also called the "supreme mind," "thought of the way," "unsurpassed mind of the way," and "the supreme intention to follow the right way." It is also described as the "seed" that leads to Buddhahood as well as the "field" in which that seed grows. Once aroused, bodhicitta is said to lead to "supreme bodhi" or the complete, unsurpassed enlightenment of Buddhahood. In this respect, bodhicitta is considered to be the deep source of all good vows, and especially the vows of a bodhisattva. The *Vairocana Sutra* says that bodhi means "understanding your own true mind," and thus bodhicitta can be understood as being a mixture of understanding and vowing.

The *Sutra on Arousing Bodhicitta* says that this state of mind can be stimulated by thinking of all Buddhas, contemplating the suffering of the phenomenal body, behaving with loving-kindness toward other sentient beings, and searching for the ultimate fruits of Buddhist practice. The *Meaning of Mahayana Terms* says that bodhicitta can be stimulated by contemplating the characteristics of impermanence and nirvana in all things, by contemplating that the cycle of birth and death is not different from nirvana, and by understanding that the true mind is none other than the bodhi mind.

The *Treatise on Bodhicitta* says that bodhicitta is stimulated and furthered when our belief in its existence is without doubt, when we have developed great compassion, when we have understood the deep meaning of the Buddha's teachings (especially his prajna teachings), and when we choose ourselves to take the highest path and not follow lower teachings. Ultimately, bodhicitta is a state of mind that lies beyond all lakshana (characteristics), and in this it is sometimes compared to a samadhi state wherein the knowing and the knower have completely merged.

BOUNDLESSNESS

Once bodhicitta has been stimulated (or found), the mind begins to open into a realm that is no longer bound by the delusions of self. Boundlessness means "without limit," "infinite," "unimpeded," "unconstrained." When the limitations of the separate self begin to disappear, the mind opens into boundless states that can be roughly described under the four headings below.

The state of boundless causes. The causes here are mental or spiritual. As we come to understand our true place in the universe, the desire to help others arises almost of itself. When we understand the consequences of selfishness and the illusions it creates, we cannot help but feel a greater unity with other sentient beings and thus want to be of benefit to them. Selflessness naturally replaces selfishness and gives rise to the boundless good causes that follow.

The state of boundless conditions. As we begin to develop bodhicitta and expand our minds, we will almost certainly realize that the conditions among which we exist are also without limit. We will come to fully appreciate the great number of sentient beings that exist within the universe and the immensity of time and space. Understanding these boundless conditions helps us appraise ourselves more rationally as it stimulates us to want to be a beneficial part of them.

The state of boundless results. As our minds open to the vastness of the reality in which we find ourselves, we will begin to reap many good "fruits" or results from the seeds we have planted in the past. Since our view of the world is no longer confined to the narrow concerns of a deluded self, we will find that we have gained access to the infinite powers of reality as it truly is. The boundless results that flow from this eventually lead to Buddhahood.

The state of boundless virtue or merit. An opened mind stands before the truth in a state of joy and peace. The boundless merits that result are usually described as follows: peaceful sleep uninterrupted by bad dreams; a consistent attitude of kindness toward others; help from higher beings; the tendency for adverse circumstances to turn out well; a shining complexion; and tranquility at the time of death.

Bodhicitta arises naturally in the course of Buddhist practice. Like all truth, it is not something that can be thrust upon us, nor is it something that can result from someone else's persuasions. We can stimulate it in ourselves by contemplating the compassion of the Buddha or by thinking deeply of the circumstances in which we find ourselves, whatever they may be. As we begin to recognize the boundless states described above, we will almost certainly feel the urge to enter them more fully. This urge is marks the deepening of bodhicitta.

THE FOUR BOUNDLESS STATES OF MIND

Bodhicitta is the basis of the four boundless states of mind and it can be described either as a vow or a realization. The rough outline of the realization has been described above. The vow or profound deepening of understanding that often accompanies this realization will be described below.

Boundless loving-kindness. Boundless kindness, or boundless loving-kindness, is the feeling of caring deeply about others, or the realization of how profoundly we already do care about them. In the *Mahaparinirvana Sutra*, the Buddha describes this feeling as "what a mother feels for her child." Many Buddhist sutras say that wisdom without loving-kindness is in danger of becoming "demonic." No intellectual attainment can replace the basic human feeling of love for others and the disposition to be kind to them.

The *Treatise on the Perfection of Great Wisdom* says that there are three basic kinds of loving-kindness: the first is loving-kindness arising from understanding the conditions in which sentient beings live and suffer; the second is loving-kindness arising from understanding the teachings of the Buddha; and the third is loving-kindness that arises from understanding the Buddha himself.

Buddhist texts recognize many kinds of loving-kindness.

- Active and negative loving-kindness. Active loving-kindness entails "starting goodness where there is none" or "fostering goodness where there is some." Negative loving-kindness means "not starting evil where there is none" or "stopping evil where there is some."
- Emotional and unemotional loving-kindness. Sometimes emotional resonance is called for and sometimes it is not. If we are wise, we will know which method is best suited to the situation at hand.
- Direct and indirect loving-kindness. Sometimes we can bring the most benefit to someone by working behind the scenes. At other times, our direct involvement will be more effective.
- Broad and narrow loving-kindness. Sometimes we will need to do big things with far-reaching consequences, and sometimes just a very small act is all that is called for.
- Constant and momentary loving-kindness. Sometimes situations require our constant attention, sometimes just a word will suffice to change everything for the better.
- Related and unrelated loving-kindness. Sometimes our contribution will be called for because we have a prior relationship with someone, sometimes it will be called for even though we have had no relationship.
- Enthusiastic and tranquil loving-kindness. Sometimes we will need to

exhibit enthusiasm to inspire others, at other times our tranquility will be of much greater service.

- Asked for and unasked for loving-kindness. Sometimes we must wait until we are asked before we help, sometimes we must act even when we have not been asked to do so.

If we humbly apply the Buddha's teachings to our lives, we will find that we often have sufficient wisdom to choose among these various types of loving-kindness. In all situations our goal should be to bring benefit to others and never to harm them.

Boundless compassion. Compassion in Buddhism literally means "removing the suffering of others." It is a companion to loving-kindness. The Lotus Sutra says, "Due to compassion, we help sentient beings who are beset with suffering." Compassion can be understood in much the same way as loving-kindness. In addition, Buddhist sutras often speak about "wise compassion" versus "foolish compassion." Foolish compassion is based on shallow sentiment, while wise compassion is based on a deep understanding of conditions leading to skillful acts that actually bring improvement to whatever the situation may be. An example of foolish compassion might be encouraging dependency in someone who already has a dependent personality. In the moment, it may seem that we are being compassionate by fulfilling their surface needs, though if we are wiser we will understand that such actions can only deepen their problems. All of us must learn to face the consequences of our behavior. When we foolishly try to shield others from the consequences of their actions, we succeed only in retarding their development. Spoiling children to the point that they never learn to discipline themselves is another example of foolish compassion.

Boundless joy. Loving-kindness inspires happiness in people, while joyful behavior inspires joy. The *Treatise on the Perfection of Great Wisdom* distinguishes between happiness and joy in this way: "Happiness results from pleasant conditions within the realm of the five sensory organs, while joy results from conditions within the mind. For example, a poor person may gain immediate happiness if we help him with the gift of money, but he will only gain joy if we continue in our kindness by teaching him a skill that will help him support himself in the future."

Boundless joy is sometimes also translated as "sympathetic joy" to underscore an even deeper meaning described by this word. Sympathetic joy is the opposite of jealousy. It means that rather than feel angry or depressed by others' achievements, we take joy in them. Sympathetic joy is the best cure in the world for feelings of envy. It teaches us to share in the goodness of others rather than rankle at their attainments. Buddhist masters often teach that while jealousy plants many bad karmic seeds, sympathetic joy allows us to share in the good karma of others. It is not all that difficult to give rise to this state of mind. The next time you feel yourself beset with envy, try generating sympathetic joy. As your mind opens to new horizons, you will find that you have completely transformed a negative situation into a positive and joyful one.

Boundless equanimity. The Sanskrit word for equanimity is upeksha. It means "not clinging" or "non-attachment," as well as "equanimity" and can be thought of as a close neighbor to the English word renunciation, in the sense of renouncing worldly attachments. Other English words for equanimity are "even-mindedness," "equal-mindedness," "impartiality," and "unbiasedness." In Buddhist texts in English, the words even-mindedness and equal-mindedness are often used in place of equanimity, while impartial and unbiased typically are not since these last two words have long histories of their own. In Chinese, the word for equanimity (*she*) is closely associated with the concept of giving, since deep "non-attachment" often leads to giving.

The *Abhidharma-kosha* says that equanimity is characterized by "even-mindedness, straightforwardness, and an absence of anxiety or excitability." Mind Only Buddhists say that equanimity is characterized by "tranquility," and that it is a product of diligence and of having disentangled oneself from states of greed, anger, and ignorance. The *Mahayana Samantha Vipassana* says that equanimity is a synonym for the "middle view," which is a synthesis of worldly and ultimate truths.

Equanimity is sometimes also identified with the fifth through the eighth samadhi states (see chapter 6) in which the form realm has been transcended, and thus also the positive, negative, and neutral sensations of the second skandha. Perfect equanimity, then, is a characteristic of deep consciousness, since shallower, sensory levels of awareness are conditioned by the realm of forms.

Equanimity is a significant aspect of the four boundless states of mind, for without it, we may become "greedy" concerning our acts of loving-kindness, anxious about our acts of compassion, or form attachments to our acts of joy. For these reasons the Buddha taught on many different occasions that we must use equanimity in our efforts to overcome delusion and that we should teach people who are new to the Dharma to undertake their studies with equanimity uppermost in their minds. Though enthusiasm can be a good thing for beginners, it must not be allowed to tip over into fanaticism, rigidity, or a trance-like acceptance of the Dharma, for traits that are themselves unwise will not readily lead to wisdom.

If our feet are bound, we will not be able to walk. Similarly, when our minds are bound by attachments and biases, we will find it difficult to learn new things. Equanimity is an inner state that we must experiment with and learn for ourselves. The ancients said, "Great equanimity leads to great (spiritual) gain, while small equanimity leads only to small gains." Boundless equanimity means that we no longer see any deep difference between "the mind, the Buddha, and all sentient beings." This awareness depends on having a profound grasp of the Buddha's teachings on emptiness, for if we understand that no thing has a self-nature and that all things come into being only through other things, we will also understand that reality is far deeper than the appearances of any of its parts.

The four boundless states of mind can be described separately, but should be understood as a well-integrated whole. All of them work together to open the mind's potential for compassion, joy, and even-mindedness. While each of these states is essential to the others, loving-kindness is normally considered to be the guiding light of them all, for without loving-kindness the core of decency and profound concern for others is simply missing. The *Treatise on the Perfection of Great Wisdom* says, "Loving-kindness is the true boundless state of mind. It is like a king, while the other states are like subjects of the king."

HOW TO AROUSE THE FOUR BOUNDLESS STATES

The four boundless states of mind are a result of successful Buddhist practice and will arise naturally of themselves. Nevertheless, they are often thought of as vows or as states of mind that we can strive to achieve. The very desire to arouse these states of mind is itself an indication that we have already begun to realize them. When growth within consciousness becomes conscious, it is difficult to say precisely where the difference between a vow and natural development lies.

Buddhist texts provide us with some techniques that can aid us in establishing these states of mind. First, they say that we should try often to understand other people's points of view, for as we increase our understanding of others, our feelings of loving-kindness naturally will increase. To truly understand ourselves, we must understand that the needs and feelings of others are not so different from our own. Second, they say that we should strive to treat all sentient beings equally and not make distinctions between friend and foe, family member and stranger, Buddhist and non-Buddhist. All of us are together drowning in the "sea of suffering" that is life in this world. When we treat all sentient beings fairly and with loving-kindness, we begin removing one of the most basic causes of all suffering. Third, Buddhist texts remind us that the four boundless states of mind must be informed by wisdom, for whenever we act unwisely, we turn away from bodhicitta, the enlightened mind that is the deep and original source of these four states.

The *Flower Garland Sutra* says, "By constantly practicing gentleness and patience under insult, we will become peacefully established in loving-kindness, compassion, joy, and equanimity."

REPENTANCE

The ancients used to say, "People are not saints, how can they be expected to never err? When we correct our mistakes, we have done something great." A life without mistakes is pleasant to imagine, but impossible to live. Profound human goodness is based upon a healthy appraisal of the self and a willingness to change for the better. If we are unable to recognize our own transgressions, we will simply not be able to grow spiritually and morally. All of us break the five precepts from time to time—and these transgressions are to be taken seriously—and yet breaking a precept is not the end of the world. Once we have recognized our mistake, we correct it and go on. If we cannot understand this process or refuse to accept it, we are in danger of entertaining a serious wrong view, for if we believe that whatever we do is justified or that we are somehow above living a moral life, it will not be possible for us to make the changes that are necessary to spiritual progress. Wrong beliefs like this can be compared to an illness for which there is no cure. No matter what we do, our illness only becomes worse. Right views are essential to the practice of Buddhism, and indeed to all spiritual paths, for if our basic views are wrong, our thoughts, speech, behavior, and purpose in life will also be wrong.

Buddhist sutras sometimes say, "Do not fear the appearance of a thought. Fear only being tardy in understanding its consequences." Buddhist practice is not based on repression or fear, but on a healthy recognition of the complexity of the human condition and the need to monitor our thoughts and actions, especially as they relate to other living beings. Once we recognize an error in our behavior, it is essential that we repent what we have done and determine not to repeat the act. Repentance is like clean water, for it can wash our minds of wrong views, pride, and ignorance. To err without repentance is to compound a problem many times by layering it over it with self-serving excuses that harm us by clouding our reason and causing us to repeat our transgressions.

THE BUDDHIST VIEW OF SHAME

Repentance is based on the feeling of shame. Most of us do not like to feel ashamed, and yet there are times when we simply must. Rather than hide from this disturbing emotion, is it not better to listen to it and follow its deep promptings? Many Buddhist thinkers have said that the most serious hindrance to spiritual growth is to lack a sense of shame, for if we have no sense of shame we simply will not be able to recognize our mistakes, much less correct them. Ironically, a person with a well-developed sense of shame actually has much more to be proud of than a proud person who has no sense of shame. The former will grow throughout his life, while the latter will only stagnate. It takes courage to entertain feelings of shame and to admit that there is no other way out of them except through repentance.

The *Abhidharma-kosha* distinguishes two sides to the feeling of shame—the recognition of the harm we have done to ourselves and the recognition of the harm we have done to others. The *Northern Parinirvana Sutra* says that having a sense of shame prevents us from harming both ourselves and others by our foolish actions. Mind Only Buddhists say that a sense of shame is one of the most important traits a spiritual aspirant can have, for a sense of shame is like a catalyst that strengthens all of the other basic qualities that lead us to the truth. The *Middle-length Discourses of the Buddha* says that a sense of shame is one of the seven "saintly traits" that are essential to the attainment of Buddhahood. The seven traits are confidence in the Dharma, moral restraint, shame, repentance, listening to the truth, practicing the truth, and wisdom.

People who lack a sense of shame are sometimes compared in Buddhist texts to trees whose bark has been removed. Though they may stand tall for a time, before long they will wither and die. The *Samyuktagama* says that if human beings were incapable of shame then none of us would recognize our obligations to our "parents, brothers, sisters, wives, husbands, spiritual communities, teachers, or elders" and that we would become "like animals."

To try to live a spiritual life without a well-developed sense of shame is virtually impossible, for the promptings of our consciences are signs of wisdom as surely as the tranquility that results from following them. To fail to recognize our own tendency to err is to be blind to that very part of ourselves that is most in need of spiritual attention. For this reason, the *Sutra of Bequeathed Teachings* says, "A sense of shame is truly magnificent."

THE BUDDHIST VIEW OF REPENTANCE

Once we have recognized an error and felt ashamed of our behavior, it is time to repent. Repentance involves seeking forgiveness and committing ourselves to not repeating the act. The *Sarvastivadan Vinaya* says that repentance requires us to admit our mistake to those whom we have offended and ask for their forgiveness. The *Platform Sutra of the Sixth Patriarch* says that repentance requires that we first admit that we have done something wrong and then vow not to repeat the act. Buddhist sutras often remind us that the ordinary mind that functions within the sensory realm is filled with impure thoughts and tendencies and that hardly a moment goes by that most of us are not committing some sort of transgression against the truth. These same sutras also remind us, though, that we should not fear our transgressions, but only our tendencies to ignore them, for whenever we experience shame and are sincerely repentant for what we have done, we lessen the bad karma that was generated during the initial act. In this vein, our minds can be compared to clothes that inevitably become dirty during the day. If we wash them at night with the clean water of repentance, then we will be able start the next day fresh. If we do not wash them, then our impurities will accumulate and become much more difficult to remove.

Repentance can also be compared to weeding a garden. Though we may plant many good seeds, if we fail to weed the ground around them, they will be strangled almost as soon as they germinate. Or we may compare repentance to a raft that helps us carry a heavy stone across a stream. Without the raft of repentance, we will find it very difficult to move the heavy stone of our karma to the shore of enlightenment. Repentance can also be said to be like a medicine that cures what ails us, a lamp that allows us to see the darkness of our own behavior, a wall that protects us from the wild, a bridge that leads to enlightenment, or an ornament that simply makes our characters appear more beautiful to others.

Buddhist sutras sometimes compare human transgressions to salt that has been thrown into drinking water. Though we cannot remove the salt from the water, they say, we can improve the quality of the water by adding more clean water to it. In this metaphor, the act of adding clean water to salty water signifies our repentance, while the drinkable water that results from this dilution signifies a lessening of our karma.

None of us should fear our feelings of shame or confuse them with low self-esteem or a lack of self-respect. Indeed, gaining a healthy sense of shame is one of the quickest of all routes to high self-esteem and self-respect, for once our appraisal of our self is based on the truth, we will no longer waste time in muddled states of mind founded on the delusions of pride and ignorance. Once we have felt the prick of conscience and recognized the error of our ways, we will have gone half of the way toward cleansing our minds of the negative tendencies that started the problem. As soon as we have repented our behavior, we can begin to look forward to a life that has been improved by wisdom and contrition. Repentance is one of our most valuable spiritual tools, for whenever we repent, we take our worst traits and turn them into some of our best.

The *Essays on Samantha Vipassana* says, "As for repentance: even the smallest bit of goodness can overcome a million kinds of evil… just as a small spark can ignite and consume a huge quantity of fuel, so even a very small bit of goodness can lead to the eradication of great evil. Though we call this sort of goodness small, its effects can be very great and for this reason we must all learn to repent."

HOW TO REPENT

The *Samanthabhadrostahana Parivarti Sutra* says that non-monastics should pay attention to five basic ideas when thinking about repentance—not harming the Triple Gem (Buddha, Dharma, Sangha), being respectful of our parents, behaving compassionately toward others, not killing sentient beings, and reflecting often on the truth and complexity of cause and effect. Contemplating these five basic areas helps us calmly review our actions against a clear and objective standard. If we find ourselves wanting in one of them, we might ask ourselves if we have also been remiss in others. For example, if we realize that we have committed a speech error against someone, as we consider what we have done, we might ask ourselves if our behavior has been proper in the other four areas as well. Did our speech result from our lack of compassion? Is it related to a poor understanding of cause and effect? Have we recently treated others in this way? If we are honest in our answers, we will gradually learn to bring these general kinds of behavior into closer accord with the teachings of the Buddha. The sutra goes on to say that after we have examined ourselves in the light of these ideas, we should make a special effort to be mindful of six other kinds of behavior that should be practiced every day—helping others, fulfilling all of our responsibilities, making donations, speaking compassionately, being grateful for what we have, and using our mistakes to bring us closer to the Dharma.

After we have identified an act of misconduct, admitted it to the person we have offended, and clearly apologized for it, we should redouble our efforts to conform to the kinds of behavior mentioned above. These actions will dilute the karma of our initial offense, help us guard against future offenses, and teach us how to use our mistakes to grow and develop. Rather than stew in the misery of unresolved emotions and damaged relations, is it not much better to be honest and move forward? Human beings are blessed with good memories, the ability to learn from their mistakes, and the power to communicate with each other. When we communicate compassionately with others in these ways, we do much to help the entire human community improve itself, for our honest admission of fault will surely have a good influence on others.

Tiantai Buddhists describe three important areas of thought and behavior that can help us understand both what kinds of actions should be repented and how to repent them. The first area is moral restraint, which is defined as not harming others. If we harm other sentient beings, we should repent our actions. To guard against further mistakes, we should work harder to understand how our behavior affects others and why it is best not to violate their rights, their privacy, or their self-respect. The second area is positive moral behavior, or helping others. Once we have learned not to violate others, we may begin to think about how to help them. We can do this by making donations to our temples, sharing our time with those in distress, teaching, and so on. This sort of positive behavior plants many good karmic seeds and thus is a very beneficial way to make up for past offenses. The third area mentioned by Tiantai Buddhists is more philosophical. It is based on a deep understanding of dependent origination, impermanence, and emptiness. By making progress in understanding these profound concepts and applying them to our lives, we gradually learn a kind of behavior that transcends the self. This sort of behavior brings only benefit to the world.

If the offense we want to repent is serious or involves people (or other sentient beings) to whom we cannot apologize because they have died or moved away, we can repent before an image of the Buddha or a great bodhisattva, a monk or nun, an elder or mentor, or to a concerned friend (the community of monks and nuns in the case of a monastic). The *Commentary on Repentance and the Four Part Vinaya* says that when we repent in any of these ways, there are five other things that we should also do. In the *Commentary*, these five things pertain to monks and nuns, but it is good for all of us to consider them. The first is to invite the presence of all Buddhas everywhere. The second is to chant a sutra or dharani. The third is to confess our misdeed. The fourth is to promise never to do it again. The fifth is to follow whatever instruction we are given by our elders, or in the case of lay followers, to deeply consider the comments of our friends. If these steps are carefully followed, we will plant good karmic seeds and move closer to a day when we will be able to forgive ourselves for whatever it is we have done. (In addition to these practices, Buddhist temples are very likely to offer repentance services that are open to the public.)

Repentance is important both for ourselves and for others, for it helps us clear our consciences and come to understand human problems on a much deeper level. Successful acts of repentance deepen our characters and increase our feelings of compassion and loving-kindness. As they chasten us toward greater honesty, acts of repentance also help us understand the fullness of the human condition and the complexities of human behavior, for only after we have understood our own failings will we be fit to understand those of others.

How do we know when we have repented enough? Surely, clinging to feelings of misery and shame can be no better than clinging to the deluded excuses that might prevent us from admitting our mistakes in the first place. Once we have decided to repent something that we have done, how do we know when to stop? One way to know is to be aware of our inner sense of balance. Most of us can tell when our desires have become excessive; if we find ourselves wallowing in feelings of remorse or guilt, we may conclude that we probably have been spending too much time looking backward. Another way to know is through examining our emotions. If we have fully plumbed our feelings and have truly gained a profound understanding of the conditions that led to whatever it is we are repenting, then we probably should begin putting the issue behind us and moving forward in a positive manner. Clinging to sadness is no better than clinging to anger or greed. The third way to know is to consult the awakened mind within, for this level of awareness allows us to transcend ourselves and all that we may believe to be true about ourselves. "On a cloudless night, the heavens are open and the moon reflects in a thousand streams." The awakened mind is always present. When the clouds of delusion are blown from it, its light reflects on everyone who turns toward it. When our feelings are pure and our minds clear, the infinite light of the Buddha simply shines upon us, and this light will tell us when we have repented enough.

THE BENEFITS OF REPENTANCE

Sincere acts of repentance not only lessen bad karma, but they also provide us with many positive benefits. Many Buddhist sutras remind us that people who are willing and able to repent their misdeeds make rapid spiritual progress. In addition to this, the sutras say that people who are willing to repent will always find themselves near to good people, always be welcomed by others, be unafraid of large groups, earn good reputations, and quickly develop bodhicitta.

The Buddha gave us many teachings because the human condition is understood differently by everyone. And yet all of us have a human mind, a human heart, and a human conscience. When these things are turned toward understanding the human condition, they always succeed for the roots of the human condition lie in the mind itself. Acts of repentance allow us to free ourselves from the dead weight of the past. They help us see ourselves in the light of present truths. And they help us learn from our mistakes so that we do not repeat them in the future.

SHARING

Sharing in Buddhism connotes reciprocity or returning to others the benefits that we have received from society, from our parents, teachers and friends, or from our spiritual studies. An important part of Buddhist practice, sharing can be compared to dispersing seeds that will give rise to good plants in the future. It can also be compared to using the flame of one candle to light many others. Acts of sharing help other sentient beings, but they also help the one who gives, for when we share we generate good karma and protect ourselves against narrow-mindedness, stinginess, and greed. Acts of sharing generally arise from a sense of gratitude and an understanding of the interconnectedness of all things. They may involve our time, money, emotional responsiveness, skills, material goods, knowledge, or wisdom. At an even deeper level, acts of sharing allow us to transfer some of our virtue or "merit" to others. Deep transmissions of Buddhist truths are always "mind to mind" transmissions. When we honestly share ourselves with others, we transmit some of our mind to them.

The *Short Prajna Sutra* says, "Understanding that there is no dharma that can be shared is the right way to share complete, unsurpassed enlightenment." This statement teaches us not to cling to acts of kindness as it reminds us that ultimately there is nothing that can be clung to anyway. The sutra goes on to say that when we cling to acts of sharing, we create only "a poisonous turmoil," for kindness with strings attached always tangles base and pure emotions and thus "poisons" itself with greed and anger.

As we think about the subject of sharing, it is beneficial to remember how much the Buddha shared with us. Those of us who are steady in Dharma practice will surely understand how much our lives have been improved by the Buddha's teachings. Our receptivity to his teachings can also be thought of as a kind of sharing, for his gift has no value unless there is someone to receive it. Sharing, thus, is always a two-way street. Sometimes we give and sometimes we receive. The discussion below will be clearer if we are aware of this.

The *Flower Garland Sutra* says that there are three basic levels of sharing or reciprocity. The first is the sharing of the bodhi mind. At this level, we receive a "cause," such as a Buddhist teaching, and attain the "result" of that teaching by understanding it and implementing it in our lives. Our response to that cause is conceived of as a kind of sharing or "returning the favor." If we learn something from a book we are reading, to take another example, that learning is the result of our openness and ability to share in the knowledge received. The second kind of sharing mentioned in the *Flower Garland Sutra* is sharing with other sentient beings. In this form of sharing we acknowledge all that others have done for us and then give of ourselves in return. The third kind of sharing is called "real sharing" or "sharing reality." "Sharing reality" means that we use some particular occurrence to understand (or explain) the deeper principles that underlie it. A friend's death, for example, may help us to understand the brevity of all life and, indeed, of all things. A small act of kindness may help us to understand the general importance of being kind in everything that we do. When we learn from our mistakes and come to understand and correct the deep-seated tendencies within us that produced them, we have "shared reality" with ourselves. When we teach these lessons to others, we have shared reality with them.

The great Buddhist master Huiyuan (334-416) explained this same three-part division in a slightly different way. He said that sharing of the bodhi mind means that we use all that we have learned from our practice to seek even purer levels of understanding. When we act upon teachings of the Buddha, we enter into a sort of feedback relationship with the bodhi mind. As we continuously learn more about it, our consciousness is continuously raised and purified. Concerning the second kind of sharing, Huiyuan said that when we share with sentient beings, we use all that we have learned from Buddhist practice to deepen our commitment to them as we purify our intentions toward them. Finally, he said that "sharing reality" means that we direct all of our virtue and merit toward realizing the deep Buddha nature of all things.

The fifty-two stages leading to Buddhahood described in the *Flower Garland Sutra* contain ten stages that are called the "ten stages of sharing." These ten stages (the thirtieth to the fortieth stages) immediately precede the ten bhumi stages of an advanced bodhisattva and by this placement demonstrate the fundamental importance of sharing as part of a complete spiritual path. As we progress in Buddhism, we may be tempted from time to time to want to keep our spiritual merits to ourselves. And yet, as soon as we attempt to do this, we begin to cling to that level of practice and to generate a sort of "spiritual greed" that completely inhibits further progress. The joy and wisdom that we gain from Buddhist practice must be shared with others, for if we do not share our achievements, a severe narrowing of consciousness will result. All sentient beings ultimately are one. When we cling to limited truths, we prevent ourselves from rising to higher levels of awareness.

The *Diamond Sutra* teaches us to "vow to save all sentient beings" even as we realize that "there are no sentient beings to be saved." This is a profound truth. It tells us that on the one hand pure actions must spring from a compassionate heart, while on the other hand our pure minds must recognize that all of the individual characteristics that seem to define sentient beings are empty. True sharing, then, is more a description of deep reality than a simple spiritual technique or prescription for human behavior. Just as deep vows are founded more on understanding than on will power, so deep sharing is most of all a result of having attained a profound understanding of the Buddha's core teachings.

The first of the ten stages of sharing mentioned in the *Flower Garland Sutra* is marked by the willingness to save all sentient beings even as one realizes that "there are no sentient beings to be saved." The second stage is marked by what is called "incorruptible sharing," which means that our willingness to share does not decrease or become perverse or counterproductive. The third stage is marked by our acceptance of the teachings of all Buddhas and our desire to become like them. The fourth stage is marked by our willingness to share our virtues or merits with everyone everywhere. The fifth stage is marked by our attainment of inexhaustible virtue or merit. The sixth stage is marked by our being always in conformance with our own best instincts or "roots" and by our willingness to share these virtues with others. The seventh stage is marked by equanimity and our ability to treat everyone equally. The eighth stage is marked by our attainment of the "mark of the Tathagata," which means that we are able to transcend the mundane concerns of this world without abandoning it. The ninth stage is marked by non-clinging and non-obstruction, which means that we no longer cling to anything or are hindered by negative character traits. The tenth stage is marked by our attainment of the "illimitable Dharma realm," which means that we are beginning to enter into the inconceivable realm of the omnipresent Buddha mind.

Sharing, thus, can be conceived of as an act of giving to others or as a state of mind that has expanded to the point that others are automatically included in all of its concerns. At this level of all-inclusiveness, sharing becomes what is sometimes called "transfer of merit," or the conscious giving of spiritual wisdom and virtue to others. This level is difficult to conceive if our thoughts are wholly rooted in the material world. Once we realize, however, that the minds of sentient beings are even more basic than the phenomena that temporarily characterize them, we will discover that when merit is transferred, nothing is really transferred, for this "transfer" is based solely upon consciously awakening to the foundation of all things. This is why kind and compassionate thoughts and intentions can be so powerful. If our minds are filled with pure and loving intentions, we actually communicate with others on a level that is far deeper than any phenomenal mark or condition. The loving-kindness inherent in this sort of sharing is much deeper and stronger than any word, expression, material gift, or form that we can conceive of. This is the level of reality that Buddhist practice is designed to help us attain. Once we begin to "share" in this marvelous level of truth, we naturally will want to share—or "transfer"—what we have discovered with others. This natural feeling of wanting to share the bounty of the "storehouse of the Tathagata" is what lies at the center of the ten stages of sharing mentioned above. Whenever we live amid truths that transcend ourselves, we will discover not only that we want to share them, but also that we cannot help but share them, for these truths simply are more basic and real than all of the artificial distinctions that seem to carve out a "you" or a "me."

The *Lotus Sutra* is speaking of this level when it says, "I vow to transfer this virtue to all things so that I and all sentient beings can attain the Buddha way." A traditional vow that has been used for centuries by monks and nuns in China also refers to this level of reality, which is so much deeper than the individual, when it says: "I vow to seek for myself neither the bounties of this human realm nor of the heavenly realm... but only those of the bodhi mind. I vow to attain highest, complete enlightenment together with all other sentient beings in the Dharma realm."

THE SIX PARAMITAS

Though Buddhism has long been recognized as being one of the world's great religions, it has unique features that clearly distinguish it from other religious belief systems. While the world's other major religions have a supreme being and a direct line of causation leading all the way back to the origin of the universe, the Buddhist world view is much more holistic. In Buddhism, human life and the phenomenal universe are subsumed within the same great totality, while all change is described as arising from the operation of dependent origination. This is why Buddhists speak of "beginningless time" and of space that has "neither an inside nor an outside." Followers of other religions generally expect to attain good health, long life, prosperity, and a contented family life by praying to a supreme intelligence. The psychology underlying this basic attitude all too often is based on human weakness, and as such, it often leads to superstition, fanaticism, and greed. Rather than contribute to human psychological growth and development, this underlying attitude very often leads only to spiritual impoverishment. Buddhism avoids this problem since its fundamental beliefs are based on a firm understanding of karma and the laws of cause and effect.

The teachings of the Buddha constantly emphasize the importance of understanding the deep truths that underlie all events, and in this they help us not only develop our innate wisdom, but also to understand the most profound levels of conscious being. By opening the vast storehouse of insight that already lies within us, Buddhist teachings explain the deep mysteries that underlie the rising and falling of all phenomena in the universe. They lead us from ignorance to wisdom and from bondage to freedom. They show us how to redirect our attention from the insignificant affairs of the brief life of a single individual to the vast and timeless unity of all things. Buddhist practice is based on the joyful realization that the liberation of the self depends entirely on our ability to bring benefit and joy to others.

Buddhist teachings on cause and effect show people how to help themselves and others at the same time. The Buddha taught selflessness, compassion, humility, and generosity in such a way that our practicing of these virtues leads inexorably to the betterment of all sentient beings, including ourselves. Buddhism is neither materialistic nor judgmental, and thus Buddhist practitioners learn to look within themselves for the causes and conditions that obtain in their lives. The Buddha taught an objective standard that helps human beings understand who and what they are, and in this he is like a doctor who provides a sick patient with a good medicine that will cure his illness. Unfortunately, too many people fail to understand the deep teachings of Buddhism. While they may understand and even respect some of the superficial injunctions of the Buddha, they all too often do not have a clear understanding of the benefits that derive from his teachings nor why the Buddha taught them in the way that he did.

Mahayana Buddhism teaches that the salvation of the self can only be attained through behavior that also saves others. The most succinct expression of this ideal can be found in the six paramitas. *Paramita* is a Sanskrit word meaning "to the other shore." The six paramitas teach those behaviors that will lead both the self and others across the river of delusion to the "other shore" of enlightenment.

The six paramitas are generosity, restraint, patience, diligence, concentration, and wisdom. The paramita of generosity teaches us to help ourselves by opening our hearts to others. The paramita of restraint helps us find freedom by teaching us to control harmful behaviors. The paramita of patience teaches us strength by showing us how to control our anger. The paramita of diligence teaches us the joy that can be found by making steady progress toward our goals. The paramita of concentration teaches us how to find deep fulfillment through living a life founded on profound awareness. The paramita of wisdom teaches us how to understand the deep sources of both our behavior and our consciousness. The six paramitas are virtues that help both ourselves and others at the same time by allowing all of our acts to spring from a mind that is calm, compassionate, and wise. I will discuss each of the paramitas in greater detail below.

THE PARAMITA OF GENEROSITY

In Buddhism *generosity* means to use compassion and wisdom to bring benefit to others. In the deepest sense of the word, this means that we share everything we have with others. People who understand generosity are the richest people in the world, while people who are mean-spirited and selfish are the poorest. Generosity can be thought of as a kind of sowing of seeds. If we have sowed no seeds, how can we expect to reap a harvest? If we never give anything to others, how can we expect to receive anything in return? As the *Treatise on the Perfection of Great Wisdom* says, people who want cool shade must understand that first a tree which can provide shade must be planted. Generosity is much like that—if want to be happy and content in future lives we must first plant the seeds of good actions in this life.

Being generous is like putting money in the bank. It is a way to protect ourselves against the future. The *Sarvastivadan Vinaya* says, "When all of our good karma is used up, we must fall into lower realms." This world is not permanent and everything must come to an end. If we have not done any meritorious deeds in this life, how can we expect to achieve a good rebirth? We come into this life empty-handed and we leave this life empty-handed. All that we have is our karma. Our next life will be entirely conditioned by what we have done in this life. For this reason, it is very important to begin planting the seeds of goodness now.

The *Treatise on the Perfection of Great Wisdom* says that acts of "pure generosity" are performed without pride, stinginess, or regret. It also says that pure generosity flows from a "pure mind that understands and believes in the workings of cause and effect; that empathizes with the recipient; that does not look for rewards in this life but understands that benefits will accrue in future lives."

Being generous provides us with more security than anything else we can do because the good karma that we generate by our generosity can never be taken away. As the verse says, "For each seed that falls to the ground, one hundred seeds can be harvested." People acquire wealth as a reward for acts of generosity that they have performed in the past. Using wealth in a way that brings long-term benefit is a sign of wisdom, for the money that we have only helps us now and in the future when we use it for the benefit of all sentient beings.

There are many different kinds of generosity, including material, emotional, and intellectual generosity. Whatever form it takes, generosity is always characterized by a profound sharing of the self with others. Since the confining limitations of the self are themselves an illusion, it is very important to understand that acts of generosity—which transcend these limitations—benefit the "self" fully as much as they benefit others. Since most people find it very easy to do things for themselves but difficult to do them for others, in the beginning of our practice it can be helpful to think of generosity as something that benefits mainly the self. If we fully understand the ways in which generosity helps us, we will be far less likely to overlook this very important spiritual virtue.

Generosity is the beginning of our profound acceptance of others and the basis of our capacity to help them. If people are tired, hungry, and poor, we must first help them overcome these conditions before we can expect them to grow spiritually. The *Lotus Sutra* says, "First hook them through their desires, then lead them to the wisdom of the Buddha." The paramita of generosity is principally concerned with helping others by using expedient methods, and as such it tends to be much more concerned with conditioned phenomena and less with the unconditioned phenomena that characterize the highest levels of the bodhisattva path.

Almost anyone with a healthy mind and a functioning conscience can perform acts of generosity, and yet only someone with great wisdom can be generous without also giving rise to feelings of jealousy, anger, possessiveness, and greed. Generosity that belittles others or makes them lose respect for themselves is counterproductive and not part of good Buddhist practice. When we give out of pride, a desire for fame, or to force others to be in our debt, we are only ensnaring ourselves more deeply in delusion, while bringing more harm than good to the recipient of our "kindness." Pure generosity that does not generate negative emotions is an art that requires both self-knowledge and an understanding of the ways of the world. In many Buddhist sutras, pure generosity is described as being "selfless generosity that does not cling to form," or "generosity that does not cling to characteristics (lakshana)."

Generosity helps others the most when it is pure, but even tainted generosity can bring benefit to us, because it teaches us how to become more pure by going beyond our instinctive needs to cling to what we own. The *Rain of Treasures Sutra* says, "Generosity helps us overcome three bad characteristics: stubbornness, envy, and mean-spiritedness." Nearly all human misery is caused by the three poisons of greed, anger, and ignorance. The most basic form of greed is to cling ungenerously to the self. The *Sutra on Good Behavior and Good Fortune* says that when we are greedy we become as slaves, for our selfish desires serve only to bind us more tightly to our narrow fixations. Greed makes us want more when we already have enough. It causes fathers and sons, brothers and sisters, and friends to fight with one another when they would benefit far more by cooperating. There is no other practice more effective than the practice of generosity for overcoming greed and the many negative tendencies that always follow in its wake, for generosity helps us look beyond the narrow considerations of the moment to the timeless presence of the goodness within us all.

Though intellectually we may find it easy to understand the importance of generosity, most of us still find it emotionally very difficult to give to others. In Buddhism, it is the mind that must teach the emotions. When we force ourselves to behave as we should, great spiritual energy is generated. Through a process that combines reason and practice, we will gradually learn to educate our emotions and bring them into line with what we know intellectually to be true. This is why it is often said that people who truly understand generosity understand that helping others is the most profound way of all to help ourselves.

Indeed, when we are given the opportunity to be generous toward someone, we should feel grateful, for that person has given us a valuable chance to grow both spiritually and emotionally. When a bodhisattva acts generously, he or she should experience great joy, for a bodhisattva should understand that each and every act of kindness, in some small way, raises the consciousness of all sentient beings everywhere. The *Upasaka-shila Sutra* says, "If we give clothing, we will be rewarded with beautiful forms. If we give food, we will be rewarded with great strength. If we give lighting, we will be rewarded with good eyesight. If we give transportation, we will be rewarded with physical comfort. If we give without any expectation of a reward, we will never lack for anything."

The *Treatise on the Sutra of Committing to the Bodhi Mind* says, "If we give flowers, we will be rewarded with the seven flowers of realization. If we give incense, we will be rewarded with the spiritual fragrance of morality, meditation, and wisdom. If we give fruit, we will be rewarded with the fruits of successful practice. If we give food, we will be rewarded with a long and healthy life. If we give clothing, we will be rewarded with pure forms and our regrets will be eradicated. If we give lighting, we will be rewarded with the Buddha eye that can see the true nature of all things. If we give elephants, horses, and carriages, we will be rewarded with the supreme vehicle of supernatural understanding. If we give valuable ornaments, we will be rewarded with the eighty subtle physical signs of a Buddha. If we give valuables, we will be rewarded with the thirty-two marks of a great person."

The *Treatise on the Perfection of Great Wisdom* says, "If we give food and drink, we will receive strength, health, and happiness. If we give clothing, with we will be rewarded with a virtuous heart, a knowledge of the difference between right and wrong, and with a healthy body and mind. If we give living quarters, we will be rewarded with all manner of wonderful buildings and be naturally awakened to the limitations of the five desires. If we give wells, springs, or other sources of water, we will be rewarded with a complete absence of hunger and thirst, and all of our desires will be satisfied. If we give boats or bridges, we will be rewarded with horses and carriages. If we give gardens and woods, we will be rewarded with great respect and all beings will seek our solace and advice."

The value of an act of generosity can never be measured on a materialistic scale. Volunteering our time, complimenting others, and teaching the Dharma are also important acts of generosity. There is a saying: "The value of our generosity depends on our intentions, what we gave, and to whom we gave it." Sometimes, even the most seemingly insignificant act can lead to great results. In China, we all know the story of the young woman who cut her hair to buy a single lamp to make an offering to the Buddha, and because of that was chosen by the emperor to become his empress. The deep value of an act of generosity lies primarily in our intentions, for if our hearts are pure and selfless, our actions will have immense influence.

The *Sutra of Past and Present Cause and Effect* says, "If we notice even a

very poor person engaged in a very small act of generosity and are gladdened by the sight, then our reward will be the same as if we had given the
thing ourselves." The value of being gladdened by seeing good things is very
important, for that sort of emotional reaction is an indication that our
minds have been awakened to a level that is deeper than any material perception or consideration. When our joys are founded on that which cannot
be seen, touched, felt, or heard, then we can know that we are being sus-
tained by the deep energies that underlie our minds and that transcend the
false appearance that we have ever been separate from others.

THE PARAMITA OF RESTRAINT

Behaving with moral restraint is a very important part of Buddhist practice.
Buddhist morality provides us with a perfect standard for the actions of our
bodies, our minds, and our speech. When people allow themselves to
become lax in their moral behavior, they invariably also become loose in
their thinking and spiritually less capable of reaching their goals. There is an
old saying: "If you do not follow the rules, you cannot be made whole." The
moral precepts of Buddhism provide us with everything that we need to
enter upon and successfully follow a wholesome and productive spiritual
path. Morality frees us from the shackles of a mind that neither understands
itself nor the world in which it lives. The *Sutra of Bequeathed Teachings* says,
"Moral restraint is the source of all freedom." The sutra also says, "Treat the
moral precepts as your great teacher."

In many ways, the moral precepts of Buddhism resemble secular law
codes, and we follow them, at least at first, in much the same way that we
follow the laws of the nations and states in which we live. In this general
sense, we can see that the moral precepts of Buddhism are not unique to
Buddhism, but that they are a necessary part of the structure of societies
everywhere, since no society can hold together if its members refuse to follow its basic rules.

The social rules of secular societies are almost always stated in the negative—they tell us what we cannot do. In Buddhism the initial stages of
moral practice—the "five precepts"—are much the same. They are negative
proscriptions that tell us how to stop harming others. The five precepts are:
no killing, no stealing, no lying, no sexual misconduct, and no irresponsible

use of intoxicants. The next level of Buddhist morality is arrived at only after we have learned to follow these basic guidelines. In the next level we are taught how to actively benefit others. The second level of Buddhist morality is the subject of this essay, the six paramitas—generosity, morality, patience, diligence, concentration, and wisdom. The six paramitas are positive virtues that tell us how to behave when we attempt to help others. In general, Buddhist morality can be summed up by the verse of the seven Buddhas: "Do no evil ever. Do good always. Purify your mind. These are the teachings of all Buddhas." The first level of Buddhist morality tells us how to "do no evil ever," while the second level tells us how to "do good always." Though there are several different levels of morality in Buddhism, at their cores each level is the same—to bring benefit to all sentient beings.

While the purpose of Buddhist morality is to bring benefit to all sentient beings, that benefit is achieved through the operation of the laws of cause and effect. Good begets good, while bad begets bad. Buddhist moral instruction teaches us to use karmic law in a way that helps sentient beings and avoids harming them. The Buddha taught that if our intentions are pure and good, then the results of our actions will be good, both for ourselves and for others. Once we understand the law of cause and effect, we become fearless when confronted with moral questions for we will have a deep understanding of how to face them properly.

There is a story that describes how in a previous life the Buddha killed one person in order to save five hundred. The story teaches us that sometimes moral behavior must be proactive and courageous. If we know how to look deeply into ourselves and are certain that our intentions spring from compassion and love, then we will acquire a wisdom and confidence in dealing with moral questions that we never had before.

The *Sutra on the Stages of Bodhisattva Development* says, "Those who uphold the precepts are joyful since their minds are not clouded with anger and regret. First, our minds must be focused on helping ourselves, then they must turn to helping others remove their fears." By learning to help ourselves spiritually and morally, we build a secure foundation from which we can wisely reach out to others. By learning to attend to the needs of others, we free ourselves from the interferences of greed, anger, and ignorance that typically cloud our minds and prevent us from making good decisions.

In Buddhism, there are very few moral transgressions that cannot be cleansed by sincere acts of repentance. Killing one's father or mother, harming a Buddha, disrupting the Sangha, or killing a saint—these are acts whose karmic consequences no amount of repentance can lessen, for each of these acts attacks the very sources of wisdom available to us in this world. Were it not for the Buddha, there would be no Dharma. Were it not for the Sangha, there would be no one to transmit the Dharma from one generation to the next. Were it not for saints, there would no one to show us the way. Were it not for our parents, we would never have been born in this world and thus never have gained the opportunity to learn anything in the first place. Harming these sources of wisdom leads to very serious and inescapable retribution. In contrast, the severity of all other moral transgressions can be lessened by sincere acts of repentance.

Buddhist practice normally entails vowing to follow the five precepts set forth by Shakyamuni Buddha. Some people are afraid to take this vow because they believe that their vows will make any future transgressions worse. This is not true. This is a seriously mistaken view. The same karmic laws apply both to those who have vowed to follow the precepts and those who have not. The advantage that we gain from vowing to follow the precepts lies in our increased awareness of what a moral transgression is and what we should do after we have committed one. If we know how to repent, we will be less burdened by guilt and more likely to understand the deep consequences of our intentional acts. Buddhist sutras sometimes compare our transgressions and the guilt that surrounds them to a heavy stone, and our knowledge of how to repent to a "Dharma raft." If we have a Dharma raft, then the heavy stone of our transgressions and guilt will not cause us to sink beneath waves of delusion.

Though it is important to have a healthy sense of right and wrong, no Buddhist practitioner should ever feel overly ashamed at having broken one of the precepts of Buddhism. Having broken a precept, we must simply recognize what we have done, repent the act, make amends for it if need be, and honestly vow not to do it again. Then we can move forward without the burden of guilt or depression that so often follows upon intemperate behavior. This is a much sounder way of dealing with the fullness of human conduct than denying the need to deal with it at all. In contrast, people who have no sense of morality, or of how to repent their misdeeds, are like people with serious diseases that have not been diagnosed. Ignorance of their condition does not lessen its seriousness. Violating the moral precepts of Buddhism is never a good idea, but it is a far less grave offense than entertaining the mistaken view that moral precepts are unimportant or that there is no need to make amends for our transgressions. Mistaken behavior can always be corrected as long as the miscreant is willing to admit the mistake. In contrast, the mistaken view that morality does not matter can be extremely serious since it can be all but impossible to penetrate a mind that has sealed itself off from the truth. The *Vinaya in Five Recitations* says, "When we know that we have erred yet are penitent, we plant good roots."

The *Flower Garland Sutra* says, "The basis of unsurpassed awakening is moral restraint." If we want to become enlightened, we must learn how to control our behavior, for if we do not, we will set in motion forces that will drag us ever more deeply into the roiling currents of the cycle of birth and death. The *Treatise on the Perfection of Great Wisdom* says, "Like a being without legs who wants to walk, or one without wings who wants to fly, those who hope for good results without upholding the moral precepts are doomed to fail."

Buddhist sutras contain many passages extolling the benefits of following the precepts and living a life based on harmlessness. The *Agamas* say, "There are five merits that accrue to all moral people: first, they achieve their most important goals; second, they attain greater material well-being and are less likely to suffer setbacks; third, their places of residence are respected by all; fourth, their reputations are good and well known; fifth, at death they will be reborn in the heavenly realm."

In the *Sutra Wherein Ananda Asks the Buddha About Fortunate and Unfortunate Signs*, the Buddha says, "Those who uphold the five precepts are fortunate people for they have nothing to fear or hide from." The *Sutra on Empowerment* says, "Those who uphold the five precepts are protected by twenty-five good spirits who hover around them and gather above the doorways of their homes and cause all things to turn out well." *The Sutra of Bequeathed Teachings* says, "Those who uphold the precepts attain many good things, while those who do not gain nothing but trouble. This point must be understood for morality is the basis of tranquility and good fortune."

Incalculable, infinite benefits accrue to anyone who upholds the moral precept of Buddhism, and yet too many people still look upon the Buddha's moral instructions as if they were intended to enslave us and cause harm. The

Buddha never said that we must do this or that we must not do that. Rather, he explained the consequences of moral versus immoral behavior and then left the decision on how to act up to us. We all have the freedom to choose how we will live, but how can anyone expect to attain spiritual and emotional liberation without living a moral life? How could it be possible that enduring happiness could ever be founded on the suffering of others?

THE PARAMITA OF PATIENCE UNDER INSULT

This world is sometimes called the "saha" world. Saha means "to endure." To simply pass our days in this world, there is much that we must learn to endure. To achieve enlightenment in this realm through Buddhist practice requires even more than that, for as Buddhists we must learn not only to endure but also to prosper and thrive spiritually. Patience is an indispensable virtue, for only when we are able to withstand human anger and greed directed toward us will we be able to be of significant benefit to others.

The Buddha taught that all delusion springs from the three poisons of greed, anger, and ignorance. While basic Buddhist practice is directed at getting us to overcome these defilements within ourselves, as we progress, we must further learn how to have a positive impact on them as they exist in others. Patience under insult might be called the "forward guard" of this endeavor, for if we are unable to withstand the inevitable malice and unkindness of others, we will never be able to do anyone very much good. Seated alone in meditation we might feel great compassion for all sentient beings in the universe, but if we lack training in the paramita of patience under insult, as soon as we go out into the world and are confronted by someone who is rude or violent toward us, our views may quickly change. The first paramita—the paramita of generosity—teaches us to reach out to others; the second paramita—the paramita of morality—teaches us how to restrain ourselves from harming others; and this third paramita—the paramita of patience—shows us how to endure the inevitable hardships that will arise as we interact with others.

In the *Sutra of Bodhisattva Precepts*, the Buddha is described as "never once becoming even slightly angry with anyone, but always being compassionate, helpful, and deeply aware." The *Sutra in Forty-two Sections* says: "Who is the most powerful? The one who can be patient under insult, for such a one is free of resentment and is respected by all." The *Sutra of Right Mindfulness* says: "People who are patient have achieved the best state of mind." The *Sutra of Bequeathed Teachings* says: "Patience is an even higher virtue than upholding the precepts or ascetic practice, for patience requires greater strength."

Patience under insult must not be confused with passivity, weakness, or cowardice, for this virtue is founded on strength and is a manifestation of wisdom. The *Sutra of Bequeathed Teachings* says: "If you cannot take as much joy from the poison of insult as you would from drinking a sweet nectar, then you cannot be called a wise person who has truly entered upon the way."

The *Treatise on the Perfection of Great Wisdom* says that there are three basic kinds of patience—ordinary patience, Dharma patience, and the patience of one who fully understands emptiness. All three of these kinds of patience come into play when we follow the paramita of patience under insult.

"Ordinary patience" can be defined as the sort of forbearance that allows us to conduct our lives in a world filled with disease, war, hardship, inclement weather, material shortages, and so on. Ordinary patience is what we normally think of as patience.

"Dharma patience" is forbearance that arises from our understanding and application of the teachings of Shakyamuni Buddha. Dharma patience relies on our understanding of such subjects as karma, dependent origination, emptiness, the four noble truths, the noble eightfold path, the three Dharma seals, and so on. When we have Dharma patience, our "ordinary patience" is raised to a new level, for no longer are we simply enduring hardship and irritation, but now we are actually seeing things in a different way. Where before we may have had the ability to control a negative response, now we have the ability to understand our situation in a completely different way and thus not give rise to a negative response in the first place.

The "patience of one who fully understands emptiness" is even deeper and more powerful than Dharma patience, for this level of forbearance is so secure the practitioner has gone beyond even the slightest feeling or thought of having to be patient at all. This level of patience is based on an understanding of emptiness that is so deep that the practitioner completely realizes that even when "phenomena" or "events" arise, nothing really has arisen. Achieving this level of patience also marks the attainment of a stage of practice called "non-regression." When a Buddhist practitioner reaches this stage, there is no longer any chance that he or she will regress to a lower stage of practice. Sometimes this level of patience is also called the "patience of non-arising dharmas" since it is based on understanding that ultimately conditioned dharmas do not actually arise at all.

The *Ekkotarika-agama* says, "A child gets his way with his tears, a woman with her beauty, a king with his power, an arahant with his self-control, a monk with his patience under insult, and a bodhisattva with his compassion." Patience under insult can be thought of as a refuge, as a kind of strength, or as a method of refining the spirit. Just as precious stones must be polished before their value can be seen, so the human spirit must learn forbearance before its deep levels of wisdom will open. As the verse says: "White jade still must be burnished by a skilled hand." When people never experience hardship and thus never learn the art of patience, they never grow to their fullest potential. In this vein, we should be thankful for the insults and injuries that people heap upon us, for these are the experiences that ultimately teach us the most. As Mencius said: "Before the heavens can bestow great responsibility on anyone, they must first test that person's resolve, work his body, starve his system, deprive him of his needs, and disrupt his life in order to strengthen his patience and improve his skills." If we want to succeed at great things, we must first learn to endure great hardship. The *Ekkotarika-agama* says: "Patience under insult is the heart of bodhisattva practice. If you can establish yourself in this, you will quickly become a Buddha."

As a method of conscious practice, patience under insult is primarily used to cure the illness of anger. The *Sutra of Bequeathed Teachings* says: "Anger is like a great fire and we must constantly guard ourselves against it and not enter into it, for there is nothing that destroys good fortune more quickly than anger." The *Fayuan Chulin* says: "Anger can cause us to lose all goodness and fall into a lower realm." It also says that anger is "the enemy of Dharma cures, a thief of the good mind, the source of harsh speech, and the great ax of calamity." The moment we become angry, our wisdom is clouded in much the same way that the sun or moon can be blocked by dark clouds. This is the reason that Master Hanshan (dates unknown, probably mid-seventh century) said, "If you want to walk the bodhisattva path, you must use patience under insult to guard your true mind."

The *Sutra of Patience Under Insult* says: "If we embrace patience and practice compassion, then life after life will pass without resentment. If our minds are tranquil, we will come to no harm." It also says: "If our lives are not tranquil, we must learn to rely on patience, for patience is like a peaceful home in which calamity never arises." And: "Patience is spiritual armor that no soldier can penetrate. It is like a great ship that can carry us across the waters of suffering; it is like a great medicine that can save many lives." *The Sutra of Mindfulness of the Right Dharma* says: "If you want to help both yourself and others, you should practice patience."

THE PARAMITA OF DILIGENCE

Diligence is a fundamental aspect of all human endeavor. Without diligence—the constant and steady application of effort to a task—nothing ever gets done. Though it may seem difficult to practice diligence at times, if we frequently look upon this important virtue as a burden, we will surely miss the great benefits that arise from it. There is a saying: "Though piles of gold may be washed in with the tide, still we must go forth and gather them." Nothing in this world is free—something never comes from nothing. Some effort is always called for in everything that we would like to accomplish. We reap what we sow.

In the *Sutra of Bequeathed Teachings,* the Buddha says to his disciples, "If you practice diligence, no task will be too difficult for you. Just as a trickle of water can wear down stone, so by your diligence you can succeed at anything."

Buddhist practice is sometimes defined as the transformation of the bad into the good, or the conversion of bad character traits into beneficial or skillful ones. This kind of fundamental change cannot possibly be effected if we are not diligent and constant in our application of effort. When the paramita of diligence is applied to the other five paramitas, a very powerful engine of goodness is brought into being. The *Treatise on the Perfection of Great Wisdom* says, "The dharma of diligence is the power behind all good actions and the source of all good practice leading to complete, unsurpassed enlightenment." The *Treatise on the Sutra of Committing to the Bodhi Mind* defines basic Buddhist practice as: "Starting goodness where there is none. Increasing goodness where there is some. Not starting evil where there is none. Ending evil where there is some." Each of these suggestions calls for the application of constant effort, or diligence. If we merely agree with these ideas but do nothing about them, our passivity indicates that we have not understood one of the most basic aspects of the Buddha's teachings—applying the Dharma to life as we live it in this world right now.

Diligence overcomes laziness, sloth, and torpor. If we find ourselves becoming lazy, the right cure is to begin emphasizing positive, beneficial activity. The *Sutra on the Practice of the Bodhisattva* says: "When householders are lazy, they run out of food and clothes. When monastics are lazy, they fail to escape from the cycle of birth and death. All good things arise from the practice of diligence."

Diligence can be understood in two basic ways—mental diligence and physical diligence. Mental diligence is the practice of being mindful about our thoughts and behavior for the purpose of eradicating our tendencies toward greed, anger, and ignorance. Physical diligence entails all of the activities that are required of our bodies to perform mental diligence. These include time spent in study, meditation, helping others, maintaining our surroundings, getting a reasonable amount of exercise, and so on. While it may be slightly better to be physically lazy than mentally lazy, it is also true that physical laziness nearly always leads to mental laziness. If we look down on our bodies and what they do, eventually they will no longer support our mind's lofty opinion of itself.

Shakyamuni Buddha achieved enlightenment before Maitreya bodhisattva because when he was a bodhisattva, Shakyamuni was more diligent than Maitreya. In the *Ekkotarika-agama* the Buddha tells Ananda: "When householders practice diligence, they have an abundance of food and clothing, their homes are spacious, and their reputations are good. When monastics practice diligence, they accomplish the goals of monastic practice. If you want to fulfill the thirty-seven conditions leading to Buddhahood, attain all of the samadhi states, understand all aspects of the Dharma, gain freedom from the cycle of birth and death, attain nirvana and the joy of the unconditioned dharmas, you should be diligent, for diligence is the foundation of all spiritual practice."

The *Moon Lamp Samadhi Sutra* says that practicing diligence brings ten great benefits:

> One, we will not be overcome by others; two, we will attain all of the benefits of Buddhist practice; three, we will be protected by non-human beings; four, we will easily remember the Dharma;

five, we will have the opportunity to hear those teachings that we have not yet heard; six, our ability to reason and persuade will increase; seven, we will attain "samadhi nature"; eight, we will have few afflictions and few problems; nine, we will obtain food easily and be able to digest what we eat without trouble; ten, we will be more like an amala flower than a stick of wood.

Diligence not only helps us overcome laziness, but it also is one of the most important factors leading to enlightenment. As we practice diligence, there are two basic things that should be kept in mind: First, we should often contemplate the sufferings of sentient beings. The *Sutra of the Lion's Roar of Queen Shrimala* describes her vows in this way:

> From this day forward until I attain enlightenment, if ever I see a lonely person, one who has been imprisoned or is ill, or who is suffering or experiencing difficulties, I will not abandon them, but instead comfort them and help them to attain freedom from their afflictions.

This sort of diligence is as much inspired by wisdom as it is certain to lead to enlightenment—the fulfillment of all wisdom—for this state of mind perceives a reality that completely transcends all individual delusion.

Second, we should often contemplate the truth of impermanence. The *Awakening of Faith in the Mahayana* says:

> You should contemplate that all conditioned dharmas of this world are transitory and that none of them lasts and that all mental activity is characterized by the constant change of one thought giving way to the next and that none of this produces anything but suffering. You should contemplate that no matter what thoughts or ideas you may have had in the past that they have all flickered and vanished like dreams. And you should contemplate that no matter what thought or idea you may be having right now that it is as transitory as a flash of lightening, and that all thoughts or ideas that may occur to you in the future are like clouds in that they suddenly may appear out of nowhere and may be transmogrified in an instant.

Most people are lazy because they do not truly understand how brief life is. Rather than treasure each moment and every breath, they tend to misapprehend the basic conditions of life and adopt the mistaken view that they can count on an endless succession of days stretching far into the distant future. As the verse of the *Admonition of Samantabhadra* says, "This day already has gone and my life has gone with it." We should approach everything we do as if "our hair is on fire" or as if "we are as a fish stranded in a shallow pool." When an appreciation for the brevity of the day is added to the tasks that we want to accomplish during it, we are renewed with the bracing knowledge that every second counts.

Sentient beings attain Buddhahood due largely to their diligence, perseverance, and determination. Patience, wisdom, generosity, and morality are very important, but if these virtues are not applied with resolute assiduousness, little will come from them. As the verse says: "Suffering makes us better people." And, "If it has not passed through a cold winter, can the plum blossom smell sweet?"

THE PARAMITA OF CONCENTRATION

The *Sutra of Bequeathed Teachings* says: "If you can concentrate your mind, there is nothing you cannot do." Most people spend most of their time caught up in the needs and desires of the five senses, and thus they rarely are able to see past the many entrancing distractions of the phenomenal world. Since they are preoccupied with the sights and sounds of the outer world, they are unable to see the pristine Buddha nature that already resides within them. Though all sentient beings have Buddha nature, very few of them are aware of it and even fewer of them ever discover it in all of its fullness. The paramita of concentration is a skill that is designed to help us turn our minds away from external distractions toward the inner peace and wisdom that already lie resplendent within us. Once we are truly able to control our minds and use them for skillful concentration, we will be able to open within us the wisdom eye that alone reveals the most profound level of human consciousness. This is the reason that Buddhists so often say, "Concentration is a great virtue, while a scattered mind leads to nothing but trouble."

The *Treatise on the Perfection of Great Wisdom* says: "Gathering the scattered mind is called 'concentration.'" To concentrate means to focus all of our mental faculties on a single point. The scattered mind is like smoke in the wind, like clouds in a storm, like thunder and lightning that appear in a moment and then are gone. The untrained mind is like a muddy stream, turbid and silt-ridden, coursing among stones and obstacles, never knowing where it will turn as it winds from this life to the next, and the next, and the next. By learning to concentrate, we gain a new perspective on this stream and from this vantage discover how to control it and use its latent powers to free it from it from its senseless wandering.

The *Sutra on the Six Paramitas* says: "Peaceful thoughts give rise to wisdom, while wisdom gives rise to further concentration. The source and basis of the enlightened Buddha mind is concentration and wisdom." The *Treatise on the Completion of Truth* says: "Concentration allows us to identify our problems, while contemplation helps us end them. Concentration is like taking a tuft of grass in our fist, while contemplation is like using a sickle to sever the bunch. Concentration is like dusting something off, while contemplation is like washing it in water."

The Sanskrit word for both "meditation" and "concentration" is *samadhi*, and thus the paramita of concentration is sometimes also called the "paramita of meditation" or the "paramita of samadhi" (see chapter 6 for a more detailed discussion of meditation and samadhi). Many people think that samadhi states can only be experienced in seated meditation. While seated meditation is the most important way to learn the samadhi states, it is a mistake to believe that the paramita of concentration can only be practiced during meditation. All of the paramitas are meant to be practiced in this world among the tumultuous sights and sounds of life as it is known to most people, and the paramita of concentration is no exception. After all, what is the value of "concentration" that functions only in a quiet room with the lights turned down? Chan Master Daowu (738–819) once told a disciple who expressed disappointment in what he perceived as a lack of instruction from his master: "If you pour me a cup of tea, don't I drink it? And if you give me something to eat, don't I eat it? If you bow to me, do I not bow back? I have never been lax in teaching you; in fact, as you can see, I have been steadfast in teaching you each and every day." The point of this story is that Buddhism must be practiced in the here and now, for any spiritual practice that allows itself to become divorced from life in this world ceases to be effective and turns quickly into mere escapism.

The essence of Chan—which means "meditative absorption"—is life itself. Eating, sleeping, working, reading, thinking, walking, talking—all of them are "Chan," and all of them should be imbued with the deepest appreciation of the fullness of our place in this world. True Chan is filled with the sights and sounds of life—spring flowers, the autumn moon, the laughter of children. It is an enormous reduction of the great art of meditative concentration to believe that it is something that must be confined to a smoky Buddha hall or that it can only be effectively practiced by old monks and nuns who have nothing else to do. Master Huineng once said, "If our minds are tranquil, what need is there for moral precepts? If our behavior is honest and clear, what need is there for meditation?" Those who are confused and groping for the truth have much to say about it, while those who really know the truth simply act in accordance with it. Profound Chan states do not refute the emotions and sensations of this world; rather, they transcend them and include them in a larger awareness.

The most common mistake made by Buddhist practitioners is that they separate their practice from their everyday lives. There has never been a Chan master anywhere who would advocate doing that. Indeed, Chan masters are renowned for their work ethic and their ability to conjoin the ordinary imperatives of daily life with the highest goals of Buddhist practice. If our behavior in this world and our responses to life are dull, how can we expect to have a vibrant and vital understanding of the teachings of the Buddha? Chan is nature itself, the deep being within, the natural response, the pure mind, the pure heart, a mind in tune with itself. There is nothing hidden in Chan and nothing that needs to be kept from others. Like a great forest, the Chan mind is open and available to all.

There is a Buddhist verse that echoes this point: "At home in your own nature and open to experience, you fulfill your ordinary being and need look nowhere else for awakening." Or: "The green bamboo all is wise while the yellow flowers all reflect the truth." If we gaze upon this world through "wisdom eyes," there is nothing that is not Chan. Before we found the way, the mountains were mountains and the streams were streams. After we found the way, the mountains still were mountains and the streams still were streams. The difference lies in how we perceive our own consciousness within the landscape that we call "this world." To the unenlightened mind, there are great differences between inner and outer and there are many needs that cry out for fulfillment. To the enlightened mind, the world and the "self" are one and our sense of who we are is as simple and clear as the call of a wood thrush across a forest pool.

If we think of meditation, or Buddhist concentration, or Chan as being something abstruse and difficult, we will miss both its true purpose and its deep essence. As the verse says: "Stopping under the tall pine, I lie with my head on a stone. Deep in the mountains there is no time, and when the winter goes, I do not recall the year." Or: "The brook trills like a long silver tongue, down the face of the mountain that stands like a pure being." Everything is Chan. Just as all of the other paramitas must be integrated with life to be effective, so the paramita of concentration is diminished whenever we think of it as something separate and distinct from life in this world.

Some practitioners believe that they must go on long retreats deep into the mountains to learn Chan. This is simply not true. Though retreats can help us gain a new perspective on life, they are not essential for the perfection of meditative practice. Huineng said: "Disentangling from outer forms is Chan, while making the inner mind peaceful is meditation." We can make our minds peaceful anywhere and at any time. And we can disentangle ourselves from outer forms without going into the mountains, for the deep meaning of "disentangling" is to be in the world without being overwhelmed by it, to participate in life without being swayed by its many negative temptations.

Basic meditative practices all involve sitting, for this is how we first learn to quiet our minds. After these fundamentals have been learned, however, it is no longer necessary to confine our meditative practice to long hours on the cushion. Deep meditative states can and should be reached even as we walk, stand, and lie down. In reference to this point, Huineng once said, "The way is found by awakening the mind. Why then do we only want to sit?" True, deep meditative attainment is characterized by the "oneness of tranquility and activity." This means that we can be tranquil even as we act and active even when we are tranquil, for at the deepest levels of the mind there are no distinctions between sitting and standing, or acting and not acting—the enlightened Buddha mind contains them all.

THE PARAMITA OF WISDOM

The *Treatise on the Perfection of Great Wisdom* says that the first five paramitas are "blind" and that they can only find their way when they are led by the paramita of wisdom. The first five paramitas can be practiced—and misapplied—by just about anyone. Without wisdom, we might practice the paramita of generosity in a way that makes someone weak or dependent, we might practice the paramita of morality in a way that is rigid and lacking in compassionate understanding of the human condition, or we might practice the paramita of diligence in a way that only leads us further from the truth. Only wisdom allows us to see how the paramitas are to be employed and for what purpose. If we do not understand the essential emptiness of all phenomena, then we will almost certainly tend to cling to our idealizations (no matter how subtle) of the forms of the paramitas without comprehending that their deep significance can only be found beyond all form.

The *Treatise on the Perfection of Great Wisdom* says: "The great vehicle of Buddhist practice is the six paramitas and the six paramitas are no different from the great vehicle of Buddhist practice." All Buddhas everywhere become Buddhas only because they have been able to attain the great wisdom necessary for achieving perfect enlightenment. If they lacked wisdom, how could they possibly gain so much? Master Yin Shun (1906–) said, "What is the use of wisdom? Wisdom is awakened to itself." The *Treatise on the Perfection of Great Wisdom* says: "Wisdom is the mother of all talents used by Buddhas and bodhisattvas and it is capable of giving birth to and rearing all manner of good things. Wisdom gives rise to Buddhas and thus it is the great mother of all things."

In Sanskrit the paramita of wisdom is called *prajna-paramita*. *Prajna* means "wisdom" (see chapter 7 for a more detailed discussion of prajna). Buddhist wisdom is the center of the mind, and it is the opening that leads to the center of the mind. Ordinary intelligence works through the compilation and comparison of data, while prajna is the seat of consciousness itself. In the *Diamond Sutra* there is a very dramatic point at which Subhuti, who has been asking questions of the Buddha, breaks down and cries. His tears indicate that he has suddenly comprehended prajna and has been filled with the emotional enormity that follows upon the awakening of the deepest levels of the mind. When the Buddha himself became enlightened, one of the first things he said was, "How amazing! All sentient beings already posses the wisdom of a Buddha, but since their minds are clouded with self-clinging, they do not perceive it."

For centuries Buddhist practitioners have strived to "transform delusion into enlightenment" by understanding the basis of intentionality and awareness. Some people are able to accomplish this transformation in a moment—so-called "sudden enlightenment"—while others may require decades to achieve a more "gradual enlightenment." Whether prajna is attained in a flash of insight or after years of hard work, it still is based on the same indescribable insight into the true nature of human awareness. Master Xuyun (1840–1959) became enlightened when he heard the sound of a tea cup breaking on the floor, while the great nun Wujinzang (precise dates unknown, probably eighth century) attained awakening at the sight of a plum flower. Though their achievements were "sudden," it is worth noting that both of these masters attained enlightenment only after having practiced Buddhism for many years, and thus, in this sense, there really is very little difference between "sudden" and "gradual" awakening.

The *Heart Sutra* says: "While profoundly absorbed in prajna-paramita, Avalokiteshvara Bodhisattva saw that the five skandhas are empty, thereby overcoming all suffering and dissatisfaction." From the point of view of ordinary intelligence, the part of our mind that functions within the phenomenal world (the five skandhas) is wholly real, while from the point of view of an enlightened bodhisattva like Avalokiteshvara it is empty, its real foundation lies deeper than any sense impression. The *Treatise on the Perfection of Great Wisdom* says: "The paramita of wisdom can eradicate darkness with light and is without stain or defilement. It brings immense benefit and serenity, and can give sight to those who are blind, and show the right path to those who are on a wrong one. The paramita of wisdom is the mother of all bodhisattvas and can help and protect all who are lonely and poor; it can overcome the cycle of birth and death and reveal the true nature of all things."

No one who does not have some sense of what is meant by the paramita of wisdom can really be said to have "right views." The paramita of wisdom includes an understanding of suffering and the way to relieve it as well as all of the other basic truths of the Buddhadharma. It teaches us how to work with the events of our lives in such a way that they help us to grow spiritually. The *Sutra of Manjushri's Questions* says: "All of our mistakes are like stains that can be washed away by the waters of wisdom." Most Buddhist practice is related to this statement in one way or another—either it helps us identify our problems, or it helps us correct them, or it shows us how to live without them. This is the function of wisdom and the basic reason that Buddhists pursue it in nearly everything that they do. As the verse says: "When our defilements have been purified, the clear moon of the bodhi mind will appear."

MAHAYANA BUDDHISM

The branch of Buddhism called "Mahayana" arose in India during the first few centuries of the common era. The word Mahayana means "large vehicle." This term was chosen at that time by Mahayana Buddhists to distinguish Mahayana teachings from Hinayana, or "lesser vehicle," teachings that the Mahayanists believed had narrowed the full import of the Buddha's original message by stressing monasticism over lay practice, benefiting the self over others, and withdrawal from the concerns of this world. The term Hinayana does not refer to any branch of Buddhism practiced in the world today and should most definitely not be associated with Theravada Buddhism, which is practiced in Thailand, Sri Lanka, Cambodia, and Myanmar. Mahayana practices were called "large vehicle" practices because they placed equal stress on the well-being of the self and others, while Hinayana practices were called "lesser vehicle" practices because they placed more stress on the well-being of the self and less on the well-being of others. Given the fact that the Buddha himself spent forty-five years teaching and helping others and that some of his most basic teachings (the five precepts and the noble eightfold path, for example) are aimed at lay followers, it is hard to reject basic Mahayana claims that the Buddhadharma is universal in both validity and application.

It is well known that the Buddha was an egalitarian thinker who rejected the caste system of his time. It is also well known that one of his most basic teachings is the equality of all sentient beings and the importance of being compassionate to all of them. The Mahayana arose in reaction to a kind of monasticism that had devolved to the point that it stressed scholarly debate over practice, seclusion and separation over community, and a social hierarchy that almost reinstituted the caste system by placing monks at the top.

Since Mahayana practice stresses the importance of all sentient beings and of living in this world, it is only natural that Mahayana philosophers have emphasized those aspects of the Buddhadharma that most assist in these goals. Mahayana philosophy is very subtle and seeks to find a way to balance the Buddha's teachings on emptiness with his teachings on compassion, his teachings on impermanence with the importance of human life, and his teachings on meditation with the importance of reaching out to others to help them when we can. Psychologically, this can be understood as balancing the human tendencies toward passivity and activity, withdrawal and participation, solitude and gregariousness. If withdrawal and passivity are stressed too much, people often become unhealthy and ineffective. If activity and gregariousness are stressed too much, people often lose sight of such higher ideals as selflessness and compassion. All religious practice must contend with these polarities in one way or another. Mahayana Buddhism stands as one of the world's great answers to the question of how to live in this world as a spiritual being without being drawn into its defilements and conflicts.

The two most important branches of Mahayana philosophy are Madhyamika and Mind Only. Madhyamika, which means "the middle view," stresses the synthesis or unity of three aspects of reality—ultimate truth (the emptiness of all phenomena), relative or conventional truth (phenomena themselves, and the imperatives they impose), and the human need to be conscious and active on both levels at once. Mind Only Buddhism says that mind lies at the bottom of all human perception and thought. This can be interpreted to mean that the "external" world is nothing more than a product of our own minds or that there is no other way in which we can know of the external world except through our own minds.

Generally speaking, Mind Only teachings are easier to understand than Madhyamika teachings since they allow us to conceive of a "mind" that underlies all things, while Madhyamika teachings would say that this mind is empty as well. Buddhists today are very fortunate since we can study all of the ancient schools and draw upon their insights without becoming entangled by any of them. Debate between these two great systems of thought might be compared to the modern debate over how to practice Buddhism in the West or how to draw on all of the Asian Buddhist traditions without diminishing any of them. One day these questions will be answered and people then will look back on these times and profit from our discussions without having to be polarized by them. This same thing can be said about the even older debate between Mahayana and Hinayana Buddhists. The question has long been settled and yet we can still benefit from thinking about it, since the psychological and emotional issues it raised shed light on the development of each human being alive today as well as on the history of the ancient world.

Since Mahayana practice arose in northern India and spread north from there into Central Asia, China, Japan, Korea, Vietnam, Tibet, and Mongolia, this tradition has come to be called the "northern" tradition in English. This is a good choice of words for it avoids creating the impression that the "southern" tradition of Buddhism that is practiced in Sri Lanka, Thailand, Cambodia, and Myanmar is a "Hinayana" tradition, which it most definitely is not. For this essay, we will continue to use the word Mahayana since the distinctions being drawn all come from the past, when this term was frequently employed.

The great Tang-dynasty monk Master Yijing (635–713) said, "When we say 'Mahayana,' we are talking about only two things—Madhyamika and Mind Only." This quote amply reveals the importance to the northern tradition of these two branches of Buddhist thought. In the sections that follow, we will look more closely at each of them.

MADHYAMIKA

The great architect of Madhyamika philosophy was an Indian monk named Nagarjuna, who lived sometime during the first centuries of the common era. Nagarjuna, who is sometimes called the "second Buddha," is remembered especially for his works the *Memorial Verses on the Middle View (Mula-Madhyamaka-karika)*, the *Treatise on the Twelve Gates (Dvadashadvaa-shastra)*, and *Twenty Songs of the Mahayana (Mahayana-vimshaka)*. The very influential *Treatise on the Perfection of Great Wisdom*, which exists only in Chinese (except for partial recent translations), is also often attributed to Nagarjuna.

Though there are many indications that he was probably not the author of this treatise, Nagarjuna was certainly the most influential philosopher in the tradition from which that book arose.

Nagarjuna is sometimes called the "second Buddha" not because he became enlightened to new Dharma teachings, but because his work shines a light that is so bright and clear into the original teachings of Shakyamuni Buddha that nearly everyone who reads Nagarjuna agrees that his understanding of the Dharma is the correct one. In a very terse style that often employs a *reductio ad absurdum* argument, Nagarjuna shows that all phenomena exist only relative to other phenomena and that each of them is thus devoid of an intrinsic essence. Though Nagarjuna claimed that all phenomena are devoid of an intrinsic essence, he did not claim that they are nonexistent. This is the heart of the "middle view," which takes a stand between the emptiness of phenomena and the presence of phenomena.

Nagarjuna also said that the phenomenal world is characterized by its manifoldness while nirvana is characterized by the absence of manifoldness and that both of these are two aspects of the same reality. This is the reason so many Buddhist masters say that "nirvana and this world are one," or that "the ordinary mind is the same as the Buddha mind," or that we "do not go somewhere when we become enlightened," but rather that we see this world with wholly new eyes. For Nagarjuna, then, and nearly all northern Buddhists who have followed after him, profound understanding of the Buddhadharma demands not that we retire from this world, but that we learn to live in it in an entirely new way. Liberation from the cycle of birth and death does not mean retreat from life in this world, but rather compassionate participation in it. Given the fact that Shakyamuni Buddha himself lived his own life in that way and that even his most basic teachings contain all of the elements of Nagarjuna's analysis, it is difficult to refute the claims of this great thinker. In the northern tradition Nagarjuna is called the "second Buddha" because people believe that he rediscovered the core of the Buddhadharma at a time when many had begun to forget the deep import of the Buddha's teachings and drift away from them into lives of withdrawal and self-absorption.

The Madhyamika interpretation of the Dharma is philosophically based upon the *Prajna-paramita Sutra* and is perhaps best expressed by the "eight negations," which were first enunciated by Nagarjuna. The eight negations are: the negation of arising, of extinction, of eternity, of ending, of unity, of difference, of arriving, and of departing. They are called "negations" because, as Nagarjuna showed, we cannot with certainty say that anything can be truthfully or absolutely described by any of these words or concepts. We cannot with certainty say that anything arises, becomes extinguished, is eternal, ends, is unified with other things, is different or separate, arrives, or departs. These eight negations were intended to deepen our understanding of dependent origination and to prevent us from clinging to absolutes in our interpretation of the Dharma, to life in this world, or to the meaning of enlightenment. Just as we cannot truly say that anything has an intrinsic essence, since everything has arisen dependent upon other things, so neither can we truly say that anything actually "arises" when it arises, or that it is truly "extinguished" when it becomes extinct. In this same vein, we also cannot say that enlightenment is "eternal" or that it is "unity" with all things or that it "arrives" or that ignorance "ends" or "departs." Nor can we truly say that an ordinary mind is "different" from the mind of a Buddha. These points constitute much more than an inventory of philosophical niceties, for if we are truly to liberate ourselves from bondage to the cycle of birth and death, we must form some sense of what that liberation might entail. The eight negations prevent us from clinging to such tired concepts as "unity" or "oneness" or of "arriving" or "departing" as we try to glimpse the ultimate goal of Buddhist practice.

The *Verse of the Two Truths* says, "All Buddhas rely on two truths to teach the Dharma to sentient beings. The first is the conventional truth of this world while the second is the ultimate truth. If people fail to understand this and fail to distinguish between these two truths, they will not be able to see to the deep core of the Buddha's teachings."

The importance within the northern Buddhist tradition of the Madhyamika interpretation of the Dharma can hardly be overstated, for these ideas had a profound and far-reaching influence on all northern schools of thought, including the Chan, Tiantai, Flower Garland, Pure Land, Esoteric, and Mind Only schools. It would probably not be an exaggeration to say that, since the seventh century, there has not been a single great northern Buddhist master who did not accept the Madhyamika interpretation of the Dharma or that there is any other philosophical development within the northern tradition that has been more influential.

In the *Kaccaayanagotta-Sutta*, Kaccaayana asks the Buddha what he means by right view and the Buddha answers: "This world, Kaccaayana, usually bases its view on two things: on existence and non-existence... Everything exists—this is one extreme. Nothing exists—this is the other extreme. Not approaching either extreme, the Tathagata teaches you a doctrine of the middle."

MIND ONLY

Mind Only Buddhism is sometimes also called *Yogachara*, which means "application of yoga." This interpretation of the Dharma accepts emptiness as a basic tenet of its philosophy, but adds to that the practice of yoga and the emphasis that all observed phenomena are nothing more than products of our minds. Mind Only Buddhism arose during the fourth and fifth centuries as a reaction, in part, to Madhyamika thought, which was considered by many to be too difficult to live with and to understand. It also arose due to the belief of its founders that the Dharma could be more easily accessed and appreciated when considered from the point of view of the human mind. The earliest and most influential Mind Only thinkers were the Indian monks Maitreyanatha (270–350?), Asanga (fourth or fifth centuries), and his younger brother Vasubandhu (fourth or fifth centuries). The most influential texts of this school are the *Yogachara-bhumi-shastra*, *Mahayanasutralamkara*, and the *Madhyatavibhaga*, which were written by Asanga, and the *Treatise on the Hundred Dharmas, Treatise on the Five Skandhas,* and the *Vimsatika* which were written by Vasubandhu.

In Buddhist monasteries, Mind Only Buddhism is often studied prior to the Madhyamika since it provides us with a single point of view and with many concepts that make it easier to grasp some of the Dharma's most difficult points. One of the trickiest questions implicit in the teachings of the Buddha is: "If there is no self, then what reincarnates?" The Buddha himself said that only our karma reincarnates, but if this is so how does this karma come to be associated with the "same" mind? In chapter 5 on the twelve links we learned that individual consciousness or the ability to discriminate among things, following death, re-arises due to an aggregation of karma that generates or produces a second, reincarnated individual consciousness, whose karma is the same as that of its former "self." The aggregation of karma continues from one life to the next, while what we think of as the "self," does not.

Though this explanation is sufficient for many people, it was not for early Mind Only Buddhists and thus they sought to answer it in a different way. To do this they added two more levels of consciousness—a seventh and an eighth—to the six levels described by the Buddha (see chapter 3). In their answer to the above question, they said that the sixth consciousness is really only concerned with coordinating sensory input, that the seventh conscious makes the decisions that generate karmic seeds, and that the eighth consciousness is the "storehouse consciousness" (*alaya vijnana*) wherein these seeds are kept. If this explanation helps us understand the Buddha's teachings better, it can be said to have value. At the same time, it can also be said that the addition of two new terms and the strong tendency to view karmic "seeds" as actual objects that are carried "in the mind" from one life to the next weakens this reinterpretation of the process of reincarnation.

The ideas of the Mind Only school should not be dismissed, however, simply because we find some of their terminology inelegant, for their perspective on the mind and what the mind can know and not know is quite compelling. They said that our individual consciousness, or our sense of owning a subjective reality, arises from kleshas or karmic seeds that are inherently tainted. It is these seeds that create the illusion of having a self that "experiences" an external world, when in fact, there is neither a self nor an external world, but only experience itself without an experiencing subject or experienced objects. All that the mind can know, they said, are concepts which are dependent on other concepts and enlightenment, which is penetration into the "suchness" or "thusness" of reality as it truly is.

Though Mind Only Buddhism was not philosophically as influential as the Madhyamika, it still had a great influence on almost all of the northern schools of Buddhism, for the literature of this tradition is replete with compelling psychological insights and analyses of human behavior. Though Mind Only Buddhism is often compared philosophically to the Madhyamika—and in its heyday during the sixth century there were many heated philosophical debates between these two schools—it would probably be better for Buddhists today to disentangle these two great traditions and think of them less as competitors and more as different ways of accessing deep levels of the Buddhadharma. Rather than emphasize their differences, we can emphasize the depths of their insights and thus gain something of great value from them both. The Madhyamika tradition provides us with one of the clearest interpretations of the philosophical aspects of the Dharma, while the Mind Only tradition provides us with some of the greatest psychological insights ever recorded.

GENERAL FEATURES OF MAHAYANA BUDDHISM

Mahayana Buddhism, or the northern tradition, as it is practiced in China today emphasizes the unity of all Buddhist practice and the importance of understanding that people always will approach the profound teachings of the Buddha in many different ways. Philosophically the northern tradition is defined by the Madhyamika and by its attempt to describe in positive terms the transcendent and omnipresent qualities of a Buddha. Before Shakyamuni Buddha became an enlightened Buddha, he was called a "bodhisattva," and thus the bodhisattva ideal, which takes the life of Shakyamuni bodhisattva as its exemplar, is central to all Mahayana Buddhism. The six paramitas discussed in this volume (see chapter 11) are the core virtues of the bodhisattva and a distinguishing feature of Mahayana Buddhism. The northern tradition is further distinguished by the great emphasis placed on lay followers, who in a more or less equal partnership with monks and nuns, seek not only to attain enlightenment for themselves, but also to do good works that will benefit the societies in which they live.

Scripturally, the early Mahayana was based primarily on the *Vimalakirti*, the *Lotus*, the *Flower Garland*, the *Mahaparinirvana*, the *Samdhinirmocana*, and the *Prajna* sutras. The *Vimalakirti Sutra* emphasizes the emptiness of all conditioned dharmas, non-duality, and the potential for even lay followers to become fully enlightened. The *Lotus Sutra* emphasizes the unity of all forms of Buddhist practice. The *Flower Garland Sutra* describes the fifty-two stages of bodhisattva practice that lead to Buddhahood. The *Mahaparinirvana Sutra* emphasizes the Buddha nature inherent in all sentient life. The *Samdhinirmocana Sutra*, which is a foundational text in the Chan school, provides a detailed description of the workings of the human mind, while the *Prajna* sutras describe ultimate wisdom and give some indication of what this world looks like to a Buddha.

Due to its emphasis on the unity of the phenomenal universe with ultimate truth, the northern tradition of Buddhism is further distinguished by a long tradition of tolerance for all forms of religious practice and a capacity to adapt quickly to social change or to move almost seamlessly from one society to another. Since the Buddha himself asked his monks to go forth and teach the Dharma in the languages that people actually spoke, it is most fitting that his teachings can be found today translated into so many of the world's languages.

At the core, the teachings of all Buddhist traditions, from whichever period of time or whichever nation, are the same. Nonetheless, people always understand ultimate truths differently. As the *Diamond Sutra* says, "The Dharma of which the Tathagata speaks cannot be held onto, it cannot be spoken, it is not a law, and it is not a non-law. And that is why all bodhisattvas understand the unconditioned dharmas differently." Unconditioned dharmas are the qualities of the enlightened mind. Historically, the ways in which people have understood the goal of enlightenment and the way to reach that goal have differed from place to place and from time to time. Rather than view these differences as divisions or schisms within Buddhism, it is more correct to view them as differences in emphasis. The different emphases of the Hinayana and Mahayana traditions were discussed above. In addition to these, Tang Dynasty China produced several other emphases within the northern tradition that have come to be known as the "eight schools." We will briefly discuss them below.

THE EIGHT SCHOOLS

The eight schools, which have long been synthesized in China into a broad, single Chinese tradition, provide us with yet another way to understand the northern tradition and what is meant by development within this tradition. The eight schools are the Three Treatises, the Tiantai, the Mind Only, the Flower Garland, the Vinaya, the Esoteric, the Chan, and the Pure Land schools. Though only the Chan and Pure Land schools still have institutionalized components in China today (i.e. temples, schools, or monasteries principally dedicated to practice within these traditions), the other six schools remain quite influential since many practitioners continue to study the literature of those traditions.

The origins of the Three Treatises school can be traced to the life and work of the great translator Kumarajiva (344–413). Based on the three treatises (or three truths of the Madhyamika—ultimate truth, conventional truth, and the synthesis of these two), this school was principally dedicated to the study of Nagarjuna's writings and the sutras and commentaries of the prajna tradition. The Three Treatises school was largely absorbed by the Chan and Mind Only schools during the Tang Dynasty.

The Tiantai school, which was founded by Master Zhiyi (561–632), is based primarily on the *Lotus Sutra* and emphasizes a balance of study and contemplation. Basic study subjects in the Tiantai tradition, which is among the most literary of all of the eight schools, include the ideas that our basic natures contain both good and bad tendencies and that one thought can contain the entire universe. Basic contemplations, which tend to cluster around Madhyamika interpretations of the Dharma, include the "one mind three views" and the "unity of the three truths" contemplations. The three truths and the three views are the three basic elements of the Madhyamika synthesis described above. During the Tang Dynasty, the Tiantai school was largely absorbed by the Flower Garland and Mind Only schools, though the writings of Master Zhiyi are still studied to this day.

The Mind Only school, which is studied today primarily for its probing psychological analyses, was discussed above. The Flower Garland school was based on the *Flower Garland Sutra* and emphasized the "unity of the six kinds of characteristics (lakshana)"—the universal characteristics (impermanence, emptiness, nirvana), the separate characteristics (individual characteristics like shape, color, aspect, etc.), similar characteristics, differentiated characteristics, characteristics of arising, and characteristics of declining. This school, whose interpretation of the Dharma was far more complex than what has been indicated here, was eventually absorbed into the Chan school.

The Vinaya school, or the school of Rules, was based on the rules set down by the Buddha for monks and nuns. The teachings of this school established the ways in which virtually all Chinese monastics behave to this day. The Esoteric, or Tantric, school, which was practiced within the imperial court during the Tang, Yuan (1206–1341), Ming (1368–1626), and Qing (1644–1911) Dynasties, did not establish deep roots in China as a whole since some of its teachings appeared to run counter to the norms of Chinese society.

Chan, the most famous of all Chinese schools, gets it name from the first syllable of the Chinese word for *dhyana* (Chinese: *chana*), a Sanskrit word that means absorption and indicates the first four of the eight samadhis (see chapter 6 for more on this). The Japanese word for Chan is "Zen." The Chan school emphasizes the importance of dhyana or concentration in everything that we do. Chan was one of the most influential of all of the Chinese schools because it was based more on meditative practice and less on scholarship and temple activities and for these reasons was better able to survive the many periods of war and turmoil that beset Chinese civilization between the end of the Tang Dynasty and the beginning of the Republican period (1911). Transmitted to China by the Indian monk Bodhidharma (470–543?), the principal texts of the Chan school are the *Prajna*, the *Lankavatara*, and the *Samdhinirmocana* sutras as well as the *Platform Sutra of the Sixth Patriarch*.

Lastly, the Pure Land school, which is based on the *Amitabha Sutra* and the *Sutra of Infinite Life*, emphasizes the triune importance of faith, vows, and practice. Practitioners of this school seek to be reborn in Amitabha Buddha's Pure Land, Sukhavati, a world-system that is more conducive to study of the Dharma than this one. Over the last one thousand years, Pure Land and Chan practice have largely merged in China. Though this merging, which centers around the meaning of the word "pure," can be quite complex philosophically, in practice it means that chanting Amitabha Buddha's name becomes a second focal point of traditional Chan practice, permitting practitioners to cultivate their spirits in this life while simultaneously preparing for their next life.

The richness of the northern tradition in China can only be glimpsed from this brief discussion, which summarizes the spiritual labors of millions of people over some two thousand years. In studying Buddhism, it is important to remember that its history in each of the other countries in which it has taken root—India, Japan, Korea, Tibet, Mongolia, Sri Lanka, Thailand, Vietnam, Laos, Cambodia, and so on—is fully as complex as its history in China. At the same time, it is remarkable that, while emphases may change from place to place, the core message of the Buddha has remained the same in all of these countries.

A main task for modern Buddhists is to discover and emphasize the underlying unity of the Buddhist tradition, even as we appreciate the richness and variety of its many manifestations. Each of the many Buddhist traditions present in the world today teaches good Buddhism and will show us how to find enlightenment. As long as our Buddhist teachers and temples are directly associated with a bona fide monastic lineage, it is nearly impossible to make a wrong choice about where to study and practice.

GLOSSARY

bodhicitta: (Sanskrit—*bodhi*—"enlightened"—*citta*—"mind") An awakened state of mind that has a good, though incomplete, understanding of reality and that clearly comprehends the goals and methods of Buddhist practice.

bodhisattva: (Sanskrit—*bodhi*—"enlightened"—*sattva*—"sentient being") A sentient being who understands the basic teachings of the Buddha and is committed to helping other sentient beings.

Buddha: (Sanskrit—"enlightened") The enlightened one. There are countless Buddhas throughout the universe. The Buddha of our world system is Shakyamuni Buddha, who lived between 463–383.

conditioned dharmas: (Sanskrit—*dharma*—"thing") All things, all phenomena; all conditioned dharmas are impermanent and empty. Compare unconditioned dharmas.

cycle of birth and death: The "beginningless" and "endless" cycle of birth, death, and rebirth. The ultimate goal of Buddhist practice is liberation from this cycle.

delusion: Views, thoughts, or perceptions derived from the mistaken notion that the "self" is real.

dependent origination: All things are caused. A fundamental teaching of the Buddha. All things "originate" "dependent" on other things. Also known as "conditioned arising" since all things "arise" due to pre-existing "conditions."

Dharma: (Sanskrit—"law") The teachings of Shakyamuni Buddha.

dharma: (Sanskrit—"thing") Things, phenomena, anything that can be named or thought of.

eighteen realms: The six roots, pus the six objects, plus the six consciousnesses.

emptiness: (Sanskrit—*shunyata*) Having no permanent or absolute aspect whatsoever. All things are empty.

five skandhas: (Sanskrit—*skandha*—"heap," aggregation") The five "heaps" of psycho-perceptual data upon which the illusion of a separate self is based.

four boundless states of mind: Loving-kindness, compassion, joy, and equanimity; profound results of conscientious Buddhist practice.

impermanence: The Buddha said that all things are impermanent.

karma: (Sanskrit—"work," "action") The law of cause and effect; all intentional acts are "causes" that generate "effects" of the same kind. This word is often used more loosely to indicate simply the result of an intentional action. "Good" karma results from actions that help sentient beings, while "bad" karma results from actions that harm sentient beings. Only a Buddha does not generate karma. All other sentient beings do.

klesha: (Sanskrit—"trouble," "defilement") Negative traits that lead to the creation of bad karma and the perpetuation of the cycle of birth and death. The six most basic kleshas are greed, anger, ignorance, pride, doubt, and wrong views.

no-self: Having no intrinsic being or "self." A synonym for emptiness.

paramita: See **six paramitas**.

prajna: (Sanskrit—"wisdom") Deep wisdom based on a profound understanding of emptiness, non-duality, and all of the teachings of the Buddha.

samadhi: (Sanskrit—"concentration") Concentration or meditative equipoise. The Buddha taught that through meditation we can realize eight samadhi states.

samsara: (Sanskrit—"journeying") The cycle of birth and death, the cycle or "journey" of existence through innumerable incarnations.

six consciousnesses: The six kinds of awareness that correspond to the six senses.

six objects: The kinds of things perceived by the sense organs; sights, sounds, smells, tastes, touch, and their influences on thought.

six paramitas: (Sanskrit—*paramita*—"to the other shore") The six primary virtues of a bodhisattva that ultimately will lead all sentient beings "to the other shore" of enlightenment; generosity, restraint, patience, diligence, concentration, and wisdom.

six senses: Sight, hearing, smell, taste, touch, and the thought processes that coordinate these.

six roots: The sense organs; eye, ear, nose, tongue, body, brain and nervous system.

three realms: The three realms of samsara—the desire realm, the form realm, and the formless realm. These realms can be directly experienced and understood through Buddhist meditation practices.

twelve nidanas: See **twelve links**.

twelve links: (Sanskrit—*nidana*—"link") The twelve stages of the cycle of birth and death; ignorance, activity, consciousness, name and form, six roots, contact, sensation, desire, clinging, existence (of karma), birth, old age and death. They are called "links" because one leads to the next.

unconditioned dharmas: The six "attributes" of the enlightened mind, or the Tathagata; timelessness, absence of delusion, agelessness, deathlessness, purity, universality, motionlessness, and joy. Compare with conditioned dharmas.

The "weathermark" identifies this book as a production of Weatherhill, Inc., publishers of fine books on Asia and the Pacific. Editorial supervision: Jeffrey Hunter. Book and cover design: David Noble. Production Supervision: Bill Rose. Printing and Binding: R.R. Donnelley. The typeface used is Bembo, with Stone Informal for display.